Evaluation with Power

INDEPENDENT SECTOR

Founded in 1980 and based in Washington, D.C., INDEPENDENT SECTOR is a national coalition of over 800 voluntary organizations, foundations, and corporate giving programs with national interest and impact in philanthropy and voluntary action.

VISION: An American society that promotes the general welfare of all its citizens and encourages active citizen participation, preserves basic freedoms, and fosters collaboration and partnerships among government, business, the independent sector, and communities.

An independent sector that is recognized for its effectiveness, responsiveness, openness, and accountability.

An organization that provides leadership toward accomplishing this vision of society and the sector.

MISSION: INDENPENDENT SECTOR is a national leadership forum, working to encourage philanthropy, volunteering, not-for-profit initiative, and citizen action that help us better serve people and communities.

For additional information, please contact

INDEPENDENT
SECTOR

1828 L Street, N.W.
Washington, DC 20036
(202) 223–8100

Evaluation with Power

A New Approach to Organizational Effectiveness, Empowerment, and Excellence

Sandra Trice Gray and Associates

Foreword by Michael Quinn Patton

Jossey-Bass Publishers
San Francisco

Substantial discounts on bulk quantities of Jossey-Bass books are available to corporations, professional associations, and other organizations. For details and discount information, contact the special sales department at Jossey-Bass Inc., Publishers (415) 433–1740; Fax (800) 605–2665.

For sales outside the United States, please contact your local Simon & Schuster International Office.

Jossey-Bass Web address: http://www.josseybass.com

A Publication of INDEPENDENT SECTOR

Library of Congress Cataloging-in-Publication Data

Gray, Sandra T.
    Evaluation with power: a new approach to organizational effectiveness, empowerment, and excellence / Sandra Trice Gray and associates; foreword by Michael Quinn Patton. — 1st ed.
        p.   cm. — (The Jossey-Bass nonprofit and public management series)
    Includes bibliographical references and index.
    ISBN 0–7879–0913–0 (acid-free paper)
    1. Organizational effectiveness. 2. Nonprofit organizations—Evaluation. I. Title. II. Series.
HD58.9.G724 1998
658.4—dc21   97–21086

HC Printing   10 9 8 7 6 5 4 3 2 1   FIRST EDITION

The Jossey-Bass
Nonprofit and Public Management Series

CONTENTS

Foreword   xi
Michael Quinn Patton

Preface   xv

Acknowledgments   xx

The Authors   xxiii

PART ONE: MAKING EVALUATION A USEFUL MANAGEMENT TOOL   1
Sandra Trice Gray

1 Ongoing Evaluation: A New Approach   3

2 Empowering Staff for Evaluation   22

3 The Board's Role in Evaluation   31

4 How Volunteers Can Contribute to Evaluation   45

5 Using Client Feedback to Improve Programs and Services   53

PART TWO: USING ONGOING EVALUATION TO STRENGTHEN KEY AREAS   59

6 Organizational Behavior and Policy   63
Astrid E. Merget, Edward T. Weaver

7 Program Effectiveness and Outcomes   74
   John A. Seeley

8 Human Resource Management   85
   Dennis R. Young, Humphrey Doermann

9 Information Management   95
   Ricardo A. Millett, Mark A. Lelle

10 Resource Development   104
    Peter McE. Buchanan, Theodore P. Hurwitz

11 Ethics and Accountability   113
    Judy Belk, Michael Daigneault

12 Adapting the Evaluation Process to the Organizational Culture   123
    Rebecca Adamson, Edward T. Weaver

13 Using Outside Evaluators   140
    Patricia Patrizi, James R. Sanders

Resource A: How the New Approach Was Developed   149

Resource B: Board Meeting Evaluation Form   161

Resource C: Board of Directors Governance Evaluation Form   163

Resource D: Board of Directors Governance Appraisal Form   167

Index   175

FOREWORD

The new vision of evaluation offered in this book grows, in part, out of the increased importance of nonprofit, independent sector organizations in addressing major social problems. President Ronald Reagan's attacks against government programs in the 1980s, especially against welfare expenditures, foreshadowed the current decline in social services funding fueled by the widespread belief that such efforts are ineffective and wasteful. Reports on effective programs have received relatively little media attention compared to the relentless press about waste and ineffectiveness. Public skepticism has turned to deep-seated cynicism. Polling data show a widespread perception that "nothing works." More damning still, in modern times, the perception has grown that no relationship exists between the amount of money spent on a problem and the results accomplished.

What is at stake, then, is not just funding for specific programs and organizations. What is at stake is public confidence in programs and organizations generally. The "nothing works" mantra gives rise to fatalism.

Why try? Why contribute? Why care?

THE ANTIDOTE TO INSIDIOUS CYNICISM

This book offers an antidote to the infectious "nothing works" mentality. What works are organizations that are effective, excellent, and empowering. Ongoing evaluation is a tool for creating, sustaining, and enhancing such organizations.

The vision of evaluation offered here, that ongoing evaluation is a means of organizational learning to support mission attainment, departs dramatically and importantly from old conceptions of evaluation in five significant ways.

Organizational effectiveness. Evaluation as a field of professional practice has focused on evaluating projects and programs. The field of organizational development has evolved parallel to evaluation, but with limited interaction between professions. This book joins recent work on organizational excellence and learning with fundamentals of empirically oriented evaluation.

In his 1988 keynote address to the American Evaluation Association in New Orleans, distinguished Minnesota state legislator John Brandl (also founding director of the Humphrey Institute of Public Policy at the University of Minnesota and veteran of the old U.S. Department of Health, Education and Welfare—HEW), challenged evaluators to move from focusing on projects and programs to focusing on the effectiveness of entire organizations. This book is the first that really addresses that challenge head-on. The vision of evaluation presented here is one where evaluation is central to the organization's culture and decision making from the board level right down to the contributions of individual staff and even volunteers and clients.

Evaluation is ongoing. The project orientation of traditional evaluation approaches made it episodic. Evaluations were conducted at project midpoints and at termination. Evaluation that is ongoing, as recommended here, can play a dramatically different role from the end-of-project accountability reports that have predominated in the past. Making the entire organization learning-oriented is a prerequisite for meaningful ongoing evaluation, not least of all because that's the only way to attract and sustain resources and support for evaluative processes.

Evaluation as learning. The end-of-project approach to evaluation emphasized rendering an overall summative judgment of merit or worth. Such judgments came to be feared and, therefore, resisted by program staff, not least of all because a singular, one-time judgment—it worked or didn't work—could seldom do justice to nuances of strengths and weaknesses, what worked well and what didn't work so well. Evaluation as learning is about improving rather than proving. This turns out to be a critical distinction. Helping those involved trust the shift from expecting punishing judgment to being part of illuminating improvements is one of the central challenges of the new vision of evaluation.

Evaluation as internal. Project-oriented evaluation was typically done by external ("out-house") and independent evaluators to maximize credibility and objectivity. This is because the primary audiences were funders external to the program. In essence, evaluation was driven by demands for external accountability. The new vision of evaluation is that the highest form of accountability is self-accountability. How well are we as an organization doing to attain our mission? Addressing that question seriously, honestly, and collaboratively within an organization involves a new vision of leadership that parallels this new vision of evaluation. It also opens up new, collaborative, and developmental roles for external evaluators.

Evaluation is doable. Traditional social science approaches to evaluation have been heavily shrouded in methodological mystique. Only evaluation experts had the technical knowledge to conduct evaluations, a proposition that made evaluation inaccessible, academic, and often irrelevant. The new vision of evaluation simplifies the process, identifies key questions, and opens up the basic logic and potential of evaluation at a commonsensical level. Evaluation must be practical and doable to be powerful. By addressing the former, the book delivers on the promise of the latter.

THE FUTURE OF EVALUATION

The future of the independent sector depends on the future effectiveness of independent sector organizations. In turn, this book suggests that the future effectiveness of these organizations depends on meaningful, useful, and practical evaluation. New calls for results-oriented, accountable organizations challenge the nonprofit sector to increase the use and effectiveness of evaluations. At the same time, indictments of nonprofit effectiveness are, underneath, also indictments of evaluation. The original promise of evaluation was that it would point the way to effective programming. Later, that promise broadened to include providing ongoing feedback for improvements during implementation. Evaluation cannot be considered to have fulfilled its promise if, as is increasingly the case, the general public perception is that few programs attain desired outcomes, that "nothing works."

Such conclusions about programs and organizations raise fundamental questions about the role of evaluation. Can evaluation contribute to increased effectiveness and organizational excellence? Can evaluation processes be empowering? This book answers these questions in the affirmative and offers an approach for realizing the new vision of evaluation as an ongoing process aimed at learning and improvement. In all these regards, it is a major contribution to both the fields of organizational development and evaluation.

September 1997   Michael Quinn Patton
The Graduate College of Union Institute
Former President of the American Evaluation Association

This book is dedicated to the "Heart of the Independent Sector"
from which this ongoing process of evaluation emerged.
And to those kindred spirits who selflessly shared their wisdom:
representatives of nonprofit organizations, foundations,
corporate giving offices, academic centers, and the evaluation
community; volunteers; members of boards; and independent
sector leadership and management consultants.

Sandra

PREFACE

As a concept, evaluation—that is, finding out whether an organization or program is doing what it was designed to do, and how well it is doing so—has obvious appeal to those who provide the resources for that activity or have overall responsibility for it. To those who do the work in question, however, evaluation often seems to draw time and energy away from their real purposes, and to measure irrelevant things for distant observers who don't understand what is happening on the ground. It becomes a high-stakes activity, and the people who provide the data generally do what they can to ensure that the results will show them in the most positive light. Wheels spin, reams of paper pile up, and the work goes on in spite of the evaluation process and almost unaffected by it except when the resultant numbers trigger a decision about funding a project. For many in the nonprofit community, *evaluation* joins *audit*, *biopsy*, and *subpoena* on the list of words they least want to hear or think about.

This is unfortunate. When evaluation is something to get through and get by at prescribed intervals, everyone loses. If you don't look, you don't see—but real results continue to build up in the real world, and programs can go so far astray they cripple themselves or (equally a problem) they can lose sight of genuine benefits that could spread far more widely if they were only noticed and publicized. Every organization—and especially every nonprofit organization—needs to learn from its ongoing experience, and the way to do that is to remove the onus from ongoing review.

BACKGROUND AND PURPOSE

INDEPENDENT SECTOR (IS), a nonprofit coalition of over eight hundred organizations with an interest in philanthropy and voluntary action, sponsored a series of focus group discussions in 1993. All told, 223 participants from almost as many nonprofit organizations met at regional Roundtable sessions in Kansas City, Chicago, Seattle, San Francisco, New York, and Atlanta, followed by national Roundtables in Minneapolis, San Francisco, and Washington, D.C. There were grant seekers and grant makers, there were men and women of a wide variety of racial and ethnic backgrounds, there were management and evaluation consultants, there were representatives of the academic community, and there were IS members and nonmembers. The project was designed to increase the level of interest in evaluation as a means of increasing organizational effectiveness, to increase the resources generally available for evaluation—the tools, methods, skills, and processes members of the nonprofit community could bring to bear—and to help organizations use the results of evaluation for learning, renewal, and institutional survival. The end product, *A Vision of Evaluation*, provided an overview of the place of evaluation in organizational life at that time, and an outline of a new approach toward using it as a means of increasing effectiveness and fulfillment of organizational missions.

The overwhelming majority of participants said that they saw a need to make an ongoing, comprehensive, and cooperative review of the organization as a system, including its results, part of the process of their everyday work. A complex and wide range of circumstances fostered this awareness. These circumstances include

- Public questioning of the performance and accountability of nonprofit organizations
- Developing expectations of high standards of ethical behavior in the independent sector
- Elevated management standards for nonprofit boards and other volunteer services

While this list is not exhaustive, it shows the environment that makes a process of continuous evaluation important for those desiring effective and relevant organizations.

The Roundtables also ran into the problem of terminology outlined earlier—the key words mean different things to different people, and often have unfortunate connotations. IS introduced the word *assessment* as an alternative to evaluation, hoping to develop a shared usage for a practice that would be constructive and beneficial at all levels of an organization, but it didn't catch on.

People continued to talk about evaluation, even though they acknowledged the word's negative baggage of judgment, interruption, and isolation from the work at hand.

This book builds on *A Vision of Evaluation*, outlining new terminology and procedures based on experience since the pioneering IS sessions. It provides a practical guide for stakeholders throughout the independent sector: grant makers, grant seekers, organization staff, volunteers, members of boards, management consultants, college and university professors teaching courses addressing nonprofit leadership and management, and users of nonprofit services. What it proposes is nothing short of a radical revision of the concept of evaluation as a way of being rather than a thing to do. It will help readers recognize the need to assemble and use information as a tool and not a threat, a source of ongoing strength and not an intermittent distraction.

INTRODUCING COEVALUATION

Independent sector organizations need constant awareness of their vision, mission, and performance. This in turn requires constant thought; otherwise, the twin pitfalls of analysis—you measure what you can count, and you get what you measure—may well warp the behavior of individuals at all levels, directing their attention away from their real mission and goals. The ideal process involves

- Asking good questions, gathering information to answer them, and sharing the information in order to make decisions based on those answers—in every aspect of organizational life, from strategic planning to daily work with clients.
- Assessing progress and changing in ways that lead to greater attainment of the mission, day by day and week by week as well as year by year, in a process of ongoing organizational learning rather than in sudden and upsetting bursts.
- Drawing everyone into the process of asking what the organization and each stakeholder can do to make the organization more effective, that is, to improve the entire system, including internal effectiveness and external results.
- Nurturing a climate of trust and developing an environment that is as risk free as possible, so people can examine why something failed with no more fear of the consequences than if they were admiring a success.
- Employing simple, cost-effective, user-friendly evaluation methods that can be adapted to meet each organization's needs and idiosyncrasies.

In other words, the ideal process is constructive and continuous and collaborative—none of which reflect concepts that leap to mind in connection with the word *evaluation* in its traditional sense. But the process is still one of evaluation, in the sense of analyzing what is happening in an organization, how it is happening, and how effectively the organization is accomplishing its mission in the context of its vision. This new process of evaluation helps an organization change and manage its way through a more complex and unpredictable environment in which it must function. This book therefore introduces a new term, *coevaluation*—literally, evaluation together—to capture the important role everyone must play in every aspect of the new continuous process.

Investment in coevaluation is time and effort well spent, saving money in the long run by making better use of limited resources. Coevaluation helps ensure the organization's health and viability in a more rapidly disconnected, changing, and shifting environment. It develops the effectiveness of an organization, empowering its stakeholders and achieving the excellence of its work. It is the essence of renewal.

The symbol provides a visual key for the change that takes place when one uses coevaluation, that is, literally "evaluation with power." In the symbol, *Ev* represents evaluation and the three *E*'s—*E* cubed, taken to the third power—represent *effectiveness, empowerment,* and *excellence.* Posted on signs and memo pads, it can serve as a constant reminder of the environment the organization seeks to create and maintain.

Ev → E³

EXCELLENCE
▲
EMPOWERMENT
▲
EFFECTIVENESS
▲
EVALUATION

Evaluation with Power covers the process of ongoing evaluation—of coevaluation—from two points of view. Part One is a practical learning tool. It explores the implications of the process for each aspect of a nonprofit organization from its staff and board of directors to its volunteers and the customers it serves, discussing the environment, the mind-set, and the specific actions needed to make coevaluation a reality. In numerous scenarios and case studies, it shows how coevaluation both improves day-to-day life in an organization and helps develop the sort of information that encourages donors to maintain and enhance funding levels.

Part Two—written before the word *coevaluation* was coined—takes a more scholarly look at the what and why of the process, bringing together voices from the foundation, corporate giving office, nonprofit organization, consultant, university, and evaluation communities. The various authors address the ongoing evaluation process as it applies to organizational behavior in general and to specific issues such as human resources, information management, and ethics, and the last chapter in the section takes up the question of what an organization committed to the internal and cooperative process of coevaluation can gain from outside evaluators.

At the end of the book, Resource A presents a detailed analysis of the INDE-PENDENT SECTOR Roundtables and their conclusions about evaluation—now called coevaluation—both what it needs to include and what the chief obstacles to it are. Resource B is a sample evaluation questionnaire designed to help an organization's board of directors assess its own meetings and the degree to which they promote its organizational mission and enhance its success, and Resource C presents sample forms for evaluating board governance in general.

All the contributors hope that this model and this book will be of use to your organization. May you turn evaluation into coevaluation on your own terms—and successfully integrate it into the everyday life of your organizational culture.

Washington, D.C.   Sandra Trice Gray
September 1997

ACKNOWLEDGMENTS

We acknowledge with appreciation the contributions of the many diverse voices of the independent sector who contributed to shaping this "ongoing process of evaluation" to empower people, to maintain effective and relevant organizations, and ultimately achieve excellence.

NATIONAL COALITION STEERING COMMITTEE

Rebecca Adamson, Founder and President, First Nations Development Institute; **Carol L Barbeito,** National Director, Applied Research and Development, Inc.; **Peter V. Berns,** Executive Director, Maryland Association of Nonprofit Organizations; **Marge Brannon,** President, Chicago Tribune Foundation; **Anne Carman,** Vice President, Development Points of Light Foundation; **Janet Carter,** Executive Director, Bruner Foundation, Inc.; **Gloria Rubio Cortes,** Vice President, National Civic League; **Allison Fine,** Executive Director, Innovation Network, Inc.; **James L. Gibson,** Regional Director, Nonprofit Organizations, National FFA Foundation; **Margaret Guerriero,** President, Amigos de las Americas; **Hedy Helsell,** Executive Director, The Center for Nonprofit Management; **Robert M. Hollister,** Director, Lincoln Filene Center, Tufts University; **Lisa Klein,** Research and Evaluation, Ewing Marion Kauffman Foundations; **Gerald Maburn,** Vice President, Planning and Coordination, American Cancer Society; **Geraldine P. Mannion,** Program Officer, Special Projects, Carnegie Corporation of New York; **Paul Mattessich,** Director, Research, Amherst H. Wilder Foundation; **Steven E. Mayer,** Executive Director, Rainbow Research, Inc.; **Ricardo Millett,** Director of Evaluation, W. K. Kellogg Foundation; **Ann**

Mitchell, Executive Director, National Council of Nonprofit Associations; **Gordon A. Raley,** Executive Director, National Assembly of National Voluntary Health and Social Welfare Organizations; **Patricia Read,** Executive Director, Colorado Association of Nonprofit Organizations; **Cynthia D. Robbins,** Vice President, Eureka Communities; **Maureen Robinson,** Director of Education, National Center for Nonprofit Boards; **James R. Sanders,** Program Director, The Evaluation Center, Western Michigan University; **Karen Simmons,** Director, Nonprofit Management Development Center, LaSalle University; **Richard Smith,** Executive Director, Support Centers of America; **Jeanne Vogt,** President, Accounting Aid Society; **Edward T. Weaver,** Vice President and Chief Administrative Officer, Ewing Marion Kauffman Foundation; **Yolanda Duarte White,** The Wilderness Society; **Dennis Young,** Governing Director, Mandel Center for Nonprofit Organizations, Case Western Reserve University.

We would also like to acknowledge with appreciation consultants **Richard Deasy, Linda Fisher, Barbara Moe,** and **Stacey Stockdill** for services above and beyond the call of duty that helped to bring this "ongoing process of evaluation" to an appropriate conclusion; and the 290 organizations that are members of the coalition supporting the principles of the "ongoing process of evaluation."

1994/95 LEADERSHIP/ MANAGEMENT COMMITTEE

Astrid E. Merget, Committee Chairperson, 1995, Louis A. Bantle Chair in Business and Government Policy, Public Administration Department, Maxwell School of Citizenship and Public Affairs, Syracuse University; **Rebecca L. Adamson,** Founder and President, First Nations Development Institute; **Kenneth Albrecht,** President, National Charities Information Bureau, Inc.; **Barbara U. Allmon,** President, H&R Block Foundation; **Gwendolyn C. Baker;** National Executive Director, YWCA of the USA; **Thomas F. Beech,** Executive Vice President, Anne Burnett Tandy and Charles D. Tandy Foundation; **Marge Brannon,** Associate Director, Chicago Tribune Foundation; **Charles W. Bray,** President, The Johnson Foundation, Inc.; **James P. Clark,** President/Executive Director, ACCESS: Networking in the Public Interest; **Sanford Cloud Jr.,** President, The National Conference; **Richard J. Deasy,** Former President, National Council on International Visitors; **Marion G. Etzwiler,** President, The Minneapolis Foundation; **Suzanne Feurt,** Program Officer, Charles Stewart Mott Foundation; **Richie L. Geisel,** President and CEO, Recording for the Blind and Dyslexic; **Nyrma Hernandez,** Former Executive Vice President, Epilepsy Foundation; **Frances Hesselbein,** President and CEO, Peter F. Drucker Foundation for Nonprofit Management; **Elizabeth Hollander,** GAP at Egan Urban Center, DePaul University; **Le Xuan Khoa,** President and Executive Director, Indochina Resource Action Center; **John Kostishack,** Executive Director, Otto Bremer Foundation; **Nancy Leon,** Executive Director, National Hispanic Leadership Institute; **Steven E. Mayer,** Executive Director, Rainbow Research, Inc.; **Ricardo Millett,** Director of Evaluation, W. K. Kellogg Foundation; **Judith A. O'Connor,** Executive Vice President, Council on Foundations; **Wendy Puriefoy,** President, Public Education Fund Network; **Patricia Read,** Executive Director, Colorado Association of Nonprofit Organizations; **Rebecca W. Rimel,** Executive

Director, Pew Charitable Trusts; **James R. Sanders,** Program Director, The Evaluation Center, Western Michigan University; **Homer Schoen**, Vice President, Marketing, National Urban League; **Michael Seltzer,** Program Officer, The Ford Foundation; **Beth K. Smith,** Former Adjunct Professor, University of Missouri, Kansas City; **John E. Taylor,** President and CEO, National Community Reinvestment Coalition; **Walteen Grady Truely**, President/CEO, Women and Philanthropy; **Michael Usdan,** President, Institute for Educational Leadership; **Edward T. Weaver,** Committee Chairperson, 1994, Vice President, Program Support Services, Ewing Marion Kauffman Foundation; and **Robert O. Zdenek,** Former Senior Program Officer, Annie E. Casey Foundation.

THE AUTHORS

Sandra Trice Gray is vice president of INDEPENDENT SECTOR, where she leads, teaches, and helps set policy with over eight hundred voluntary organizations, corporations, and foundations that are national and international in scope. She directs the IS Leadership Agenda and International Initiatives. Gray directed the exploratory and organizing phases, and established the Secretariat of CIVICUS: World Alliance for Citizen Participation, and served as interim director.

Prior to joining INDEPENDENT SECTOR, Gray was executive director of the National School Volunteer Program. She has served as a commissioner for Intergovernmental, Interagency and Community Liaison, U.S. Office of Education; assistant and policy adviser to the Undersecretary of Education; and fellow and special assistant to the Secretary of Health, Education and Welfare. Gray earlier had an extensive career as an educator and administrator on the state and local levels, including serving as the first African American to teach in the desegregated public school system in Little Rock, Arkansas.

Gray serves on several national, state, and local nonprofit boards and commissions. She is cochair of the Alliance for National Renewal and was an honorary co-chairperson of the Sustainable Communities Task Force of the President's Council on Sustainable Development. She has published articles addressing building community, business, and education partnerships, leadership, diversity, and inclusiveness, giving and volunteering, ethics and accountability, including "Values" in *Foundation News and Commentary* and a column, "Leading" for *Association Management*. She is also a coauthor of *Profiles of Excellence*.

Gray was a member of a delegation of American women leaders to the Soviet Union sponsored by the Rockefeller Foundation and was chosen as one of America's top hundred black business and professional women. She was a member of the President's Committee on Education Partnerships. She is a member of the American Management Association, the American Society of Association Executives, the National Coalition of 100 Black Women, and Women and Philanthropy. Gray is a certified association executive. She has a proven record of success in coalition building, as evidenced by this book.

Rebecca Adamson is founder and president of First Nations Development Institute. She received an M.S. in economic development from New Hampshire College in Manchester, where she also teaches a graduate course on indigenous economics in the Community Economic Development Program. Adamson serves on the board of directors of the Calvert Social Investment Fund and on the Calvert High Social Impact Board. She received the 1996 Robert W. Scrivner Award from the Council on Foundations for creative and innovative grant making as well as the National Center for American Indian Enterprise Development's 1996 Jay Silverheels Award.

Judy Belk is vice president of community affairs of Levi Strauss & Company and vice president of the Levi Strauss Foundation. Belk received a B.S. from Northwestern University and an M.P.A. from California State University, Hayward. Belk worked as public affairs manager for Mervyn's Department Stores, an operating company of the Dayton Hudson Corporation. Previously, she was director of public affairs for the Association of Bay Area Governments and Community Relations Officer for the City of Sunnyvale. Belk is on the board of directors of INDEPENDENT SECTOR and on the advisory committee of the Center for Corporate Community relations at Boston College.

Peter McE. Buchanan is president of the Council for Advancement and Support of Education (CASE). Buchanan earned a B.A. from Cornell University, an M.B.A. from the Columbia Business School, and an Ed.D. from Teachers College of Columbia University. Buchanan previously worked at Columbia University, at Wellesley College, and for Colgate Palmolive. He has served on the boards of INDEPENDENT SECTOR, the Dana Hall School in Wellesley, the Episcopal Divinity School in Cambridge, and the Wellesley College Center for Research on Women in Wellesley.

Michael Daigneault is president of the Ethics Resource Center. Previously, he was the president and founder of Ethics, Inc. Earlier, Daigneault was the executive director of the American Inns of Court Foundations. He earned a B.A. in philosophy from Georgetown University and received a J.D. and an L.L.M. from the Georgetown University Law Center. He was the graduate student adviser to the nation's first law journal devoted to legal ethics, *The Georgetown Journal of Legal Ethics.* Daigneault is the ethics columnist for *Federal Lawyer* magazine.

Humphrey Doermann is the president of the Bush Foundation. He earned an A.B. from Harvard University, where he also received an M.B.A. (1958) and a Ph.D. (1967). He was formerly director of admissions for Harvard College and assistant dean for financial affairs of the faculty of arts and sciences. Doermann is chairman of the board of the Council on Foundations.

Theodore P. Hurwitz is president of Price Charities. He received an L.L.B. (1961) from Boston University. He earned an L.L.M. in taxation from DePaul University. Hurwitz was formerly vice president for institute relations at the California Institute of Technology. Earlier, with a specialty in planned giving, he was associate vice president of development at the University of Chicago.

Mark A. Lelle is a principal and senior consultant with Community Resources Group, a firm specializing in evaluation research, strategic planning, organization development, and fund raising management. Lelle earned a B.S. in agricultural education from Ohio State University and an M.S. in agricultural education from Louisiana State University. He received a Ph.D. in resource development from Michigan State University. Lelle was undergraduate program coordinator in the department of resource development at Michigan State University.

Astrid E. Merget serves as chair of the Department of Public Administration and associate dean of the Maxwell School of Citizenship and Public Affairs at Syracuse University. In 1994, she served as senior adviser to the Secretary of the U.S. Department of Health and Human Services. Previously, Merget spent eight years at Ohio State University, where she directed the School of Public Policy and Management and spent a year as the acting dean of the College of Business. A fellow of the National Academy of Public Administration, she was elected a trustee of its board in 1987, then vice chair in 1988 and chair in 1991 until 1993. She had also been a consultant to the Committee for Economic Development, the International City Management Association, and numerous other governmental and nonprofit organizations.

Ricardo A. Millett is director of evaluation for the education department strategic planning area of the W. K. Kellogg Foundation. He received a B.A. in economics at Brandeis University, where he also earned an M.A. in social policy and a Ph.D. in social policy planning and research. He is the author of "Empowerment Evaluation and the W. K. Kellogg Foundation," in *Empowerment Evaluation: Knowledge and Tools for Self-Assessment and Accountability,* edited by David Fetterman, Shakeh Kaftarian, and Abraham Wandersman (1996). Millett has been an associate professor of research at Boston University and was formerly director of the Martin Luther King Center there.

Patricia Patrizi is an associate at both the Harvard Family Research Project and the Consortium for Policy Research in Education at the University of Pennsylvania, where she is part of study teams working on outcomes accountability and issues surrounding taking educational reform "to scale." Prior to these posts, Patrizi was director of evaluation for the Pew Charitable Trusts. Her particular expertise is in creating evaluation designs that jointly maximize authority, participation, and usefulness. Presently, she is working with a number of foundations to assess and develop approaches to evaluation.

Michael Quinn Patton is former president of the American Evaluation Association and recipient of the Alva and Gunnar Myrdal Award for "outstanding contributions to evaluation use and practice." He is the author of *Utilization-Focused Evaluation: The New Century Text* (1997), *Qualitative Evaluation and Research Methods* (1990), and *Creative Evaluation* (1988).

James R. Sanders is a professor of educational leadership and the associate director of the Evaluation Center at Western Michigan University. He earned an M.A. in educational research from Bucknell University and a Ph.D. in educational research and evaluation from the University of Colorado. Sanders has been a visiting professor at St. Patrick's College in Dublin, Utah State University, and the University of British Columbia. He has consulted with numerous school districts, corporations, foundations, government agencies, universities, nonprofit organizations, and United Ways. He has served on the board of directors of the American Evaluation Association. He is chairman of the Joint Committee on Standards for Educational Evaluation.

John A. Seeley is the president of Formative Evaluation Research Associates, an evaluation research organization in Ann Arbor, Michigan. He earned a B.A. (1965) and an M.A. (1967) at the University of Colorado and a Ph.D. (1978) at the University of Michigan. He has published articles and delivered workshops on evaluation in the United States and abroad. He is familiar with the benefits and problems of various approaches to evaluation and is a strong advocate for the use of evaluation as a significant management tool. Seeley is president of the Michigan Association of Evaluators.

Edward T. Weaver is vice president of program support services of the Ewing Marion Kauffman Foundation. He earned an M.S.W. at Washington University and a Ph.D. in public administration at the University of Southern California. He was for ten years a visiting professor at the George Warren Brown School of

Social Work at Washington University. He is vice president of the board of directors of the Camp Fire Boys and Girls, Inc., treasurer of Mid-America Care Foundation, and president of Midwest Care Centers. He is a former president of the Paramount Communications Foundation and a former member of the board of directors of INDEPENDENT SECTOR.

Dennis R. Young is professor of nonprofit management and economics at Case Western Reserve University. He serves on the governing boards of the National Assembly of National Health and Social Welfare Organizations and the International Center for Nonprofit Law and on the advisory board of the Nonprofit Leadership and Management Program of York University, Toronto. He is a consultant to CIVICUS: World Alliance for Citizen Participation. Young received a B.S.E.E. from City College of New York and an M.S.E.E. and a Ph.D. in engineering and economic systems from Stanford University.

PART ONE

MAKING EVALUATION A USEFUL MANAGEMENT TOOL

Sandra Trice Gray

Traditional evaluation is a periodic effort aimed at producing an organizational report card. Coevaluation is a way of being, an integral part of organizational culture aimed at producing continuous change and improvement. To help make the leap from one to the other, Sandra Trice Gray uses Part One to discuss the key elements of coevaluation—asking good questions, collecting information, and sharing and using that information—from a variety of points of view to make decisions. Although many readers will gain from all five chapters, others will find it sufficient to read only Chapter One and the chapter that comes nearest their own place in the organization.

Chapter One goes over the process as a whole, discussing the rationale and terminology and introducing the basic framework. It shows how adopting the process can move an organization to new levels of effectiveness, empower all its stakeholders to make a difference in the way it affects their lives, and refine its mission and the way it carries out that mission so as to produce true excellence. The concept of the Questioning Agenda presented here can turn any meeting around, allowing the participants to spend their time making a difference for the future rather than dissecting their past.

Chapter Two discusses the coevaluation process as it involves the paid staff of an organization, from the executive director to the receptionists. The chapter assesses the role of leadership both formal and informal in implementing and maintaining the ongoing, collaborative effort the new process requires. It also explores the kinds of questions that make a difference in individual and group settings.

Chapter Three turns to the board of directors. It shows how coevaluation can enhance internal board operations as well as permeate the board's approach to its organizational responsibilities, its relationship with the executive director, its own membership, and its fund raising activities. A long series of tailored questions and a separate meeting-evaluation questionnaire help focus board attention on what really matters to an effective and relevant organization.

Chapter Four shows how volunteers fit into the coevaluation process, pointing out that their position at the interface between the organization and its clientele gives them insights often unavailable to paid staff members. The chapter recasts the process and the questions from the volunteer standpoint, and it also provides guidelines for establishing coevaluation that includes volunteers.

Chapter Five underscores the basic premise that coevaluation has to be everyone's job—including participants and clients as well as paid staff, directors, and volunteers. It discusses the cost of concentrating on the deficits of participants in human service programs and ignoring their very real strengths and assets, and it shows what a program can do to capitalize on the insight and experience of its clients. Once again, it illustrates the good questions in terms useful for clients to ask and answer.

All five chapters include scenarios and case studies, providing a body of anecdote that can be used to seed the collective wisdom of an organization. People live and learn by stories, and most organizations have a raft of unfortunate stories to replace—stories about people who answered questions honestly and lost their jobs, stories about people who made suggestions and got laughed off, stories about people who called attention to problems and got blamed for them. To make coevaluation work, an organization needs new stories, stories about people gathering and using information to improve their own effectiveness and the organization as a total system. Home-grown success stories will develop soon enough as coevaluation takes hold, but until that time these will serve to reinforce the descriptions of how the method works. Wherever the reader may be in an organization's world, from director to outside observer, there are ways to introduce the coevaluation process and begin making a difference.

CHAPTER ONE

Ongoing Evaluation

A New Approach

In the nonprofit world, it is easy to fall into a pattern of thinking and acting in terms of need and problem. There is so much to do, and human, financial, and material resources are so limited, that it can seem out of place to spend less than every available scrap of time and money on the next case, the next client, the next problem to arise. When distant funders or oversight agencies demand reports, it seems an imposition. How can we stop doing the important things we're doing, just to compile a lot of numbers—to jump through a hoop for someone who ought to know how valuable we are already? At the same time, given the realities of funding and the modern social and political climate, how can we not?

For the ongoing health of our organizations, we need to set aside the hoop-jumping and bean-counting view of evaluation. As long as it is a single event or activity that comes at the end of a grant-funded project—and bears only on those organizations seeking such funding—then evaluation *is* an imposition. As soon as we turn the idea around, however, and look at the benefits strengthening of every aspect of the organization to determine how well we are doing overall to attain our mission while holding our vision, the imposition vanishes.

What we need is a new process—a cooperative, continuous, and constructive process that lets us see clearly where we are and where we are going and when, as well as how, we must change. We need a process that encompasses all its stakeholders, that is, a process whose input comes from everyone involved in or with an organization, from its funders and its board to its volunteers and the people it serves, and whose output is directly useful to those same groups. To differentiate this new collaborative evaluation from the old bean-counting variety, this book introduces a new term: *coevaluation.*

Coevaluation is the means by which an organization continuously learns how to be more effective. It provides a means of organizational learning, a way for the organization to assess its progress and change in ways that lead to greater achievement of its mission in the context of its vision. A process and not an event, it is ongoing rather than episodic. As it becomes ingrained in day-to-day operations, the participants see results in terms of improvements in their own work and the teams' achievement of outcomes, as well as the organization's functioning as a total system because of the interdependent nature of the process. Evaluation got its unfortunate image by being a report card, an after-the-fact rating that came too late to permit any improvement. Coevaluation is a tool, always in use, always opening the door to the next beneficial step.

At the same time, as a happy by-product, coevaluation develops information about results. When it is necessary to go to a funder for a new or renewed grant, an organization that engages in coevaluation will already know what it has accomplished and what it stands to accomplish with additional resources. With a clear view of its successes, learnings, and how to build on them—and of its environmental challenges and how to address them—such an organization can make a very strong case indeed for its slice of the grant maker's pie.

COEVALUATION AS LEARNING

Coevaluation involves a natural, though disciplined, use of three steps: asking good questions, gathering and reviewing information, and sharing the information to foster good decision making. The key point here is the need to ask *good* questions, questions that keep the mission central while accurately probing individual and organizational effectiveness. Such questions generate information that empowers the participants and the people in the organization to take appropriate action—seeing something clearly is the first step toward improving it. Sharing the resulting information internally and externally allows all the stakeholders to use it as they make individual and collective decisions, decisions that move the organization to new levels of excellence.

Effectiveness, empowerment, excellence: these are the results of coevaluation—that is, evaluation fully integrated into the life of the total organization.

The Nurturing Environment

For coevaluation to be a natural, disciplined process, part of the work life of an organization, the internal environment must be made as risk free as possible, so people can come together to examine why something succeeded or failed without fear of consequences. It thrives in a climate of trust, which must be promoted and nurtured by the organization's leadership.

It helps when everyone is speaking the same language. Words need to have the same meaning and to be commonly understood by all parties, especially the new paradigm's definitions for the coevaluation process. Several key points require general acceptance:

- Coevaluation is the responsibility of everyone in the organization. Everyone gathers information through good questions, shares the information, explores the possibilities, contributes to decisions. Everyone accepts the feedback coevaluation generates as a way of assessing progress, enhancing effectiveness, and continuing to learn, grow, and change.

- Coevaluation addresses the total system of the organization, its internal effectiveness and external results. At the same time, coevaluation aims for improvement rather than judgment. No one is immune, and no one who is pursuing the organization's interests is at risk.

- Coevaluation invites collaborative relationships within the organization and with external parties such as clients, community members, businesses, government, donors, funders, and other nonprofit associations. All the stakeholders seek jointly to learn how to reach excellence.

Coevaluation will flourish in an organization with these values. And the relationship will be reciprocal. Coevaluation understood and practiced in a natural and disciplined manner will strengthen and sustain such an organizational ethic. It will lead to effectiveness, empowerment, and excellence.

Coevaluation in Context

Evaluation with Power does not cover traditional evaluation, which involves many procedures and tools for instrument development, data collection, sampling procedures, and quantitative or qualitative analysis. Instead, it urges processes that can be used in organizations of any size as part of their daily routine. Coevaluation serves as an umbrella for all other forms of evaluation. Implemented on an ongoing basis, it provides the context for a holistic approach to strengthening an organization's effectiveness. Chapter Thirteen discusses ways to take advantage of the skills of specialists in the use of traditional evaluation tools. The organization that understands coevaluation as a natural and continuous learning process and integrates good questions, information collection, and shared decision making into its daily routines will be comfortable with the scrutiny of these technical performance reviews (requested by policy bodies, funders, or others), and benefit more from them than one that fears their interference. On an ongoing basis, however, most organizations need simpler processes that can be used as part of their daily routine, helping them be effective in environments of more rapid and disconnected change. This chapter presents an overview of coevaluation in use, and many of the other chapters provide further insights.

There is no mystique to coevaluation—it is simply a way of learning. We do that all the time. But coevaluation does require a bit of discipline, a bit of conscious effort at first. But then the process is as easy as 1, 2, 3:

1. *Ask good questions.* Good questions lead to effectiveness.

2. *Collect the right information.* Good and useful information to answer the questions leads to empowerment.

3. *Share the information and make decisions.* Sharing the information in a manner that strengthens the decision-making process leads to excellence in organizational performance and achievement.

Picture yourself in the recurring cycle shown in Figure 1.1. Start at 1, move through to 3 and start over again. Consider this an *effectiveness feedback process,* a process of asking for data or evidence upon which to act more effectively in your daily work.

Staff in organizations who have experienced the effectiveness feedback process report that the evaluation loop increases their appetite for information. They solicit more feedback, formally and informally, than they ever did before. They start using the results—and they stop worrying about them.

HOW COEVALUATION WORKS

Like many really good ideas, coevaluation looks simple and obvious when the bare elements are spelled out. In practice, there are some wrinkles that make it useful to analyze the process in detail.

Step 1: Ask Good Questions

Well, what *are* good questions? Good questions are appropriate and relevant to a situation, need, or concern. They are meaningful to the success of the organization. They are the ones you really want answers to—no matter what—and at the same time, they are questions that *have* answers that are credible and useful. (Unless you're in advanced geriatric research, for example, it isn't worthwhile to spend much time wondering why every day everyone gets a day older. . . .) Good questions also encourage collaboration with others, and trigger creativity, adaptation, and flexible thinking. They tend to flow from and focus attention on the organization's vision, mission, values, and ethics. Good questions look like these:

- How does my work promote or limit the organization's ability to attain its mission?

- How do I convey or not convey the organization's vision and values in my work with other employees or in my interactions with clients?

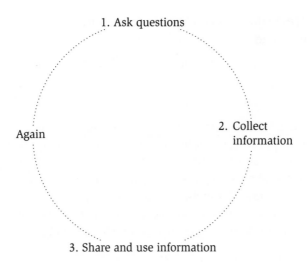

Figure 1.1. Effectiveness Feedback Loop.

- Have I helped board members know and understand our bylaws?
- Have I put proper procedures in place for ensuring compliance with all applicable laws?

Similarly, good questions arise from reflection on organizational philosophy, policies, roles, relationships, and programs.

Educators often refer to "teachable moments." Organizations have what might be called *learning moments,* when something happens and a staff member, volunteer, client, or board member recognizes significant potential for the organization to learn. While coevaluation is an ongoing process, there are natural times to create learning moments.

Questioning Standard Procedures

When a literacy center first opened, standard procedure was to assign volunteer tutors in random order as adult learners came in requesting help. Volunteers began to experience frustration, although they were not sure why. The obvious response—change the matching process—only led to more frustration. Change to what? Why? This was a learning moment. Something was ineffective; good questions were needed.

- What is happening in our matching process?
- What is working? Not working?

- What are volunteers and clients saying and feeling? What do they want instead?

- How will we know when the situation is better?

Create Learning Moments at Every Staff Meeting. Meetings are an easy way and a key entry point to introduce the new process of coevaluation into an organization. Anytime colleagues meet together there is opportunity to build or reinforce a shared meaning of evaluation as learning and to ask good, strategic questions. Consider changing the staff meeting agenda. That is, instead of the traditional items—round-robin reports, old business, new business, and so on—pose a series of probing questions at the staff meeting:

Questioning Agenda for a Staff Meeting
- Since we last met, how have we advanced the organization's vision, mission, program area plan, committee charge?
- What was the benefit to the organization? To our clients?
- What prevented us from making further progress?
- If those obstacles were removed, what would happen? If those obstacles remained in place, what could we do instead?
- What single action can we take right now to break through to a higher level of effectiveness? How would we know?
- What benefits would the organization or our group gain from having other people or other resources in our meetings? Who else should we invite? What else should we have available?
- Are you getting the information you need to be more effective? How can our staff meetings be more helpful?

One nonprofit organization planned "reflection" for the end of every staff meeting. The organization helped unemployed inner-city youth gain academic, vocational, and carpentry skills. During the reflection period, staff were asked to focus on one successful case and one case that was not as effective. The learnings from each case were discussed, not the "score."

Consider Changing the Board Meeting Agenda. Board meetings are another key entry point for modeling the new vision. They offer a prime opportunity to focus on the organization's learning capacity at the highest organization level. Using a Questioning Agenda not only provides for a more stimulating and effective meeting, but is more responsive to the needs of the organization.

Most organizations send materials and reports to board members prior to meetings. The agenda usually consists of "discussion of" the materials and reports. Consider, instead, an agenda consisting solely of questions such as these.

Questioning Agenda for a Board Meeting

- From the information you received, how well is the organization holding the vision and attaining its mission? What is the evidence?
- Are there missing pieces? Extraneous material? What could be provided instead, and in what way? What would be the benefits to the board? To the organization?
- Of the board's many responsibilities, which one are you most concerned about? Why? What would you like to be different?
- What do you see in the community or elsewhere that represents an opportunity for the organization to be more effective?

As board members become comfortable with Questioning Agendas, the reports and materials provided them will change in nature as well.

For example, instead of "progress reports" of various functions or subcommittees, "learning reports" can be submitted. These will show how staff are addressing fundamental questions and how improvements are occurring.

Searching for Excellence

Prompted by a questioning agenda, one member of an adult day care center board suggested looking at the operations of other and different day care center organizations. The information and insights would strengthen board performance, she suggested. Several other board members picked up on the idea until the guiding question became "what makes for excellence in day care center organizations?" With this context, good evaluation questions included:

- What is an excellent day care center organization? What is the evidence of excellence?
- How do successful day care organizations operate? What is the relationship of the board with the organization?
- What methods do they use to promote and sustain their success? Which methods are most effective? How do they know?
- What strategies distinguish their excellence?

Using a Questioning Agenda—while a good model of an ongoing process of evaluation—may be too dramatic a change. The meeting leader, without heightened attention, can begin the process gradually by simply asking for feedback: "Let's take some time to talk about ways we made a difference recently. What do these experiences tell us about what we did right and where we need to change?" Or simply add two or three questions to each board meeting agenda. But don't miss the opportunity of this learning moment.

Other Learning Moments. Meetings are not the only natural opportunity to practice coevaluation. Here are others:

Short-term planning. Introduce or reinforce organizational learning through the planning processes. At the end of a planning period, ask good questions on an informal basis to identify what has been learned or how programs and services might be modified or changed during the next period. Good questions might be

- What worked in our plan for the last period? Was it worthwhile?
- What was the impact on the organization?
- What did we learn that we can use during the next period?

Annual planning. The end of a program year is a good time for all members of the organization—staff, volunteers, clients, board members—to reflect and think about organizational effectiveness and ask good questions. But keep in mind that the coevaluation process promotes continuous learning. It is not a fixed point in time. Until everyone is speaking the same language and is committed to the new process of examining the organization and its results, there still may be a tendency to judge what went wrong and what went right.

Good questions could start with

- How appropriate was our plan to holding the vision and fulfilling our mission?
- What activity, program area, or plan section had the most impact? Why? Can we build on that?
- If we stopped doing X, what would happen? If we started doing Y, what would be the benefits?
- If we pushed for excellence in just one area, which will get us the furthest?
- What are our learnings from last year's plan? What are the implications for our next plan?
- What evidence will we have that next year's plan advances the organization's effectiveness?

Internal research and studies. Most organizations undertake evaluations, research projects, or studies about programs and activities. Often these studies are for a specific purpose; learning opportunities beyond the immediate need may well be overlooked. Reviewing these documents from a different, broader perspective can identify additional evaluation questions.

A client recruitment study, for example, may have addressed a nagging problem six months ago. What do the results tell you now about other organizational issues or activities, such as orientation procedures, client services, internal operations?

State, federal, and other funding reports. Coevaluation invites a collaborative relationship within the organization and with external parties as well. Asking good questions of yourself and your colleagues begins the evaluation process. Asking good questions also promotes involvement by others, invites new ideas, generates excitement, and encourages partnering beyond the work group. These new collaborations are especially critical as you collect, share, and analyze the information for answers to the good questions.

Funders of a legal advice program asked about the number of clients served from various cultural backgrounds. The agency reported accordingly. The percentages, indeed, showed that their client base, originally Southeast Asian, had become increasingly diversified over a five-year period. They regarded this as success, but carried the learning one step further. The information suggested other good questions:

- Considering our vision and the greater diversity of our clients, how appropriate is our mission statement? Our program area setup? Our organization structure, policies, staff resources?

- What do we need to change? Start? Stop?

Practice, practice, practice. Make a quick list of other natural learning moments that occur in your organization. Better yet, have *everyone* make a list.

Step 2: Collect the Right Information

If you are asking good questions to probe your daily effectiveness, you are already engaged in a process of great benefit to you and your organization.

But now you need to take the next step around the loop, the step that will empower the organization with new capacities. You need to collect the information that answers your questions.

The key is to collect the *right* information, and to do so collaboratively with others—those who have information and those who need it to be empowered to act on behalf of or improve the organization. Good questions will steer you to the right information. This section provides a helpful checklist to review before you begin collecting the answers.

Confirm the Focus of the Question. Are the questions clearly worded to focus on what you need to know? The key step is simply to ask someone else what the questions seem to mean and what kind of information they call for. Until you get used to framing unambiguous questions—and sometimes even afterward—you may be astonished at the differences in what seems obvious to different people. By vetting the questions in advance, you can greatly increase your chances of getting the information you really need.

Think Through What Having the Answers Might Mean. The results of your evaluation need to be useful. Ask yourself and your collection team: If we get this information, what will it do for us? Is having the information worthwhile? Is there value in knowing it or is it just nice to know? Are there any disadvantages to collecting the information?

Consider Who Has the Information Now. Identify the sources that need to be queried and how they can be approached. Sometimes the sources are obvious. In other cases, you will need to do some brainstorming or networking to find them—use your team, other organization members, your community. In deciding where to get information, consider the broadest possibilities first. Then winnow down.

Use the opportunity to enlist the sources themselves in your process; engage them in the effort. An easy way is to offer to share the results of your evaluation—people are much happier about providing information when they expect to learn what you have learned and what you are going to do about it. In this way you stimulate their interest in giving you good information.

As evaluation becomes part of the ongoing life of the organization, it will get easier to locate information sources. But it is always important to spend time with colleagues identifying where the best information or good answers can be found.

Identifying Good Sources

When a community foundation decided to secure answers to the question "should we focus on specific programs?" the staff decided that the collective perceptions and judgments of a number of informed respondents were the best source of information. The community foundation chose three types of resources for their information:

- *Insiders:* Those closest to the organization and its programs and activities, including executives, program staff, board members, donors.

- *Recipients:* Those organizations receiving grants.

- *Informed Observers:* Community leaders outside the foundation who know and understand its mission and have perceptions about the impact of specific foundation activities; members of the media, and those who study, teach, or write about the sector.

Decide on Collection Methods. Having determined what to ask and of whom, you need to think through how to do it. Any number of information-gathering methods are available.

Keep in mind the kind of data gathering you will be doing is *ongoing and part of a process,* not episodic or an event. Therefore, in establishing your sources and your methods, try to build in a continuing connection. Get your sources enlisted in the process by sharing your learnings and results with them. Strengthening *their* capacity to learn, as well as your own capacity, is the essence of empowerment.

The choices for information gathering are already part of your working life, for example:

- *Face-to-face interviews:* Ask clients during appointments if their needs are being met.

- *Questionnaires:* Ask volunteers to write down what they like about volunteering in your organization and recommendations they have for enhancing the experience.

- *Telephone interviews:* Have questions near your phones to ask of dissatisfied clients.

- *Files and records:* Review existing records kept by the organization to determine the cultural diversity of your client population. Also, make use of data available from other sources (such as census data) that would put the organization's work in context.

- *Group interviews:* Ask board members to talk about the quality of information being provided to them. (See the discussion of the Questioning Agenda earlier in this chapter.)

- *Observation:* Observe clients in your reception area, at your meetings, conferences: Do they actively relate to the staff?

In general, you should choose information collection methods and resources that will provide you with the most useful information and will give you what you need to make decisions. They should be the tools that you, your staff, and your evaluation partners have the time and skill to use, are within your budget, fit the culture of your organization, help others to give you the information you are seeking, and seem likely to provide information that will be viewed as credible, accurate, and useful (Stockdill and Stoehr, 1993).

Avoid Some Common Pitfalls. Double-check your decisions about the who-what-how of your information collection before you go ahead. That is, make sure your method of collection is free of bias or clues as to expected responses— the only useful information is what's real, not what people think you want to hear. Consult people who represent a variety of viewpoints, not just those that support your own opinions and ideas. Consider the potential respondents' experience, language proficiency, and access to information—and motivation to provide it—and construct questions likely to evoke their best efforts to reply. In addition, make sure the ongoing work of the organization can continue without great disruption while you are consulting internal respondents and using resources for information collection. These four precautions will greatly enhance your chances of winding up with information that is relevant and useful—and that doesn't cost more to gather than it is worth to your organization.

Plan Your Process. Whether doing coevaluation on a personal level or as part of a collaborative effort with others (inside or outside the organization), you need to plan the process and tap into the resources needed to collect information.

Schedule a preparation period, a time when you make decisions about how information will be collected, from whom, by whom, and by what date. Make a list and a time line.

Consider the skills needed for the various collection methods and the skills available to carry them out. If you (or your team) have greater skill in a particular method, you may be most comfortable choosing that method for answering your good questions. But be certain your choice is appropriate for the process, not merely comfortable. New skills and techniques may be required and may provide additional learnings.

Remember: The process of gathering information to answer important questions is *empowering*.

Step 3: Share the Information and Make Decisions

Sharing and using information gathered in response to good questions—the third part of the coevaluation process—gets you to the bottom line. It is here where the people and the process make the biggest impact, raising the organization to new levels of excellence.

Whether doing the coevaluation individually or as part of a team, you will need to:

- Summarize the data.
- Share the information.
- Make decisions and develop plans.
- Communicate your plans.
- Respond to the reactions of others.

Summarize. Summarizing the data is what makes sense of it. In its raw state the gathered data will generally exist as numbers, written responses, or verbal statements. Your task will be to pull the information out of the data—to put it all together in ways that are easily understood and meaningful to you and to others. Quantitative data are probably easiest to present—graphs, percentages, tables. Qualitative data, on the other hand, are harder to boil down into useful insights.

But you asked good questions, so the answers can be summarized around the questions. Or you will find certain themes emerging in the answers. The information will fall into and around these themes.

Take time to reflect before you summarize. Resist the temptation to rush to results. Instead, mull over the data. Review your purpose for the evaluation. Did you get what you wanted? Look at your questions and the responses. If you are missing information or if responses are not clear, you may need to return to your respondents and probe for clarification and explanation.

But probably you will have all the information you need—even more than you might think you can handle at first. That's why you need to think about it and immerse yourself in it. Shuffle it around and summarize it several different ways. This will give you the best sense of what's important and what isn't, and which responses fit together or enhance each other. It will help you determine the most meaningful way to summarize so that others will understand.

Having reflected and mulled, prepare the summary of your data. Quantify when possible; use themes with illustrative, direct, but unidentified quotes for the qualitative questions.

Share the Information. Sharing the information with others occurs twice— once when you and your team meet and compare notes, data, summaries of the data you each have, and so on. And again, after you have summarized and done preliminary analysis. Then you need to shift into a sharing and communication mode. "Here's what we learned; here's what we are proposing to do; here's where we need your help; what do you think?"

You should have involved others in the evaluation already—so joint analysis, planning, and coordinated action will be a matter of your team presenting the results and enlisting the others in enhancing and carrying out the plan of action.

"Work" the information with others. Some people see the trees in the forest, others see the forest as part of a larger landscape, still others appreciate the leaves. In other words, people think in different ways—and a good coevaluation team needs all kinds of thinkers. As you work the data, team members will see different patterns and possibilities. This is a strength of the working group, and of the collaborative evaluation process.

As part of sharing information, linkages between organizational constituencies, units, or functions will become apparent. Draw in other people from those units. Pose options with them. Develop alternative proposals and rationales based on the data and ask for reaction or support.

This sharing can be accomplished by giving affected and interested persons copies of the summarized information to review and then discuss at a meeting, or to review individually and give feedback to you in written form. Presenting the summarized information at a meeting gives everyone equal access to the information and the discussion plus an opportunity to contribute to its interpretation. Remember: Meetings are key entry points for implementing coevaluation. A Questioning Agenda for such a meeting might look like the one in Exhibit 1.1.

At this meeting a common ground is established. The group comes to a mutual understanding about the potential outcome and the evaluation results and meaning. Refinements are made, and the shared vision, mission, and values of the organization will be represented.

A written feedback approach would involve, again, providing summarized responses and results, and asking individuals to complete a feedback form such as the one in Exhibit 1.2.

The idea of "working the information" is to create ideas and possibilities. Look for connections between your potential plan and the implications for the rest of the organization. Involving others in the process makes it possible.

Make Decisions and Develop Plans. Given your own analysis and what others saw in the data, you now need to make decisions. More good questions will help you here:

- What does the information indicate needs to be started? Stopped? Changed?
- What is it we want instead?
- Who will be affected inside the organization? Outside it?
- What resources will we need? Whose help?
- What are the costs involved?
- What is the priority of action?

Develop a preliminary plan of action. Pull your report of evaluation results together after you have reviewed the data in this way. You will now have done analysis and made decisions, and you will have a good idea of what kind of actions need to be taken and who needs to be involved.

Meeting Agenda

1. Review the information: 30 minutes

2. Discuss—based on the information: 1 hour

   • What is surprising?

   • What are strengths?

   • What are issues, weaknesses, needs, or concerns?

   • Are any changes needed? If yes, in what areas?

   • How should program changes be made?

   • How can we use this information?

   • Who should be responsible for making identified changes?

   • When will program changes be made?

   • How will we know if changes have addressed the problem areas?

   • How will we inform individuals who provided information what actions
     were taken?

Exhibit 1.1. A Meeting Based on Good Questions.

Written Feedback Form

Attached is a summary of some information we collected. We would like you to review this information and answer the following questions. Your responses will help us develop a plan of action to increase organizational effectiveness.

- What is surprising in this information?

- What are strengths of this program?

- What are the issues, weaknesses, needs, or concerns?

- Are any changes needed? If so, in what areas? How should program changes be made?

- Who should be responsible for making identified changes?

- How will we know if the changes have addressed the problem areas?

Exhibit 1.2. Keeping Track.

Many kinds of action planning formats are used in organizations. If your organization uses one that is working and commonly understood by everyone, you are ahead of the game. If your evaluation is an opportunity to change or to introduce a planning technique into the organization, then design a format that includes the elements in Exhibit 1.3.

Finally, you have a coordinated plan of action. All the time spent on the steps of the coevaluation process, the building of shared understanding, and the efforts of joint planning result in a clear plan, ready and able to be implemented.

Communicate Your Plans

We are assuming that whether you are doing coevaluation as an individual or as a team, you are accountable to someone or some organizational entity, and that you have involved them in the process from the start. Communication with them has been ongoing. But there are others who need to know of your plan, most of whom will have been involved in the development of the information or in its analysis.

Your plan, along with a brief summary of the process used in reaching it, should be sent to all concerned—up, down, and across the organization—to demonstrate how the process works and involve everyone in the plan and its success. As a secondary benefit, distributing the plan also distributes the information you've discovered and develops the potential for increased effectiveness, sharing with others the capacity to learn—the power of coevaluation to move the organization forward to excellence.

Respond to the Reactions

Involvement, collaboration, and joint effort have been emphasized as essential to an effective coevaluation process. They will also help overcome the obstacles to learning and change. Linda Fisher, in *A Vision of Evaluation*, talks about a "few simple truths about people and process" (1993, p. 34):

- *People commit themselves to what they help create.* The time you take in working with others to develop good questions, to collect the information, to plan the action steps—all this results in a heightened interest and commitment level. It helps, too, to establish mutual trust and credibility between all parties.
- *Evaluation results must be seen as accurate, credible, and useful to the organization if learning and change are to take place.* In *The Fifth Discipline*, Peter Senge (1990) defines learning as "the enhancement of the capacity to produce results that really matter." He believes that people are intrinsically inquisitive about things they care about. You have the unique opportunity to tap the intrinsic curiosity of your organization's constituencies—its staff, board, volunteers, clients, funders—all those who care deeply about the organization's mission.

Sample Planning Format

- *Outcomes:* The overall results you want to achieve.

- *Action Step:* The tasks or activities required to accomplish the outcome.

- *Rationale:* The reason for the action step; keeps the focus on the outcome.

- *Responsibility:* Who will take the action; who else will be involved in making it happen.

- *Timing:* Dates and deadlines for action completion. Include a midcourse review for checking on progress and action step revisions.

- *Resources Required:* Time needed, costs, involvement of others, and so on.

- *Evidence of Success:* Criteria for successful completion of action step.

Exhibit 1.3. Information Needed for Action.

Senge adds that while an organization's mission or shared vision is important, so too is its common understanding of current reality. Information is useful to the organization when it enhances that common understanding.

• *Resistance is normal and to be expected.* Resistance is understandably strongest when evaluation results influence funding and survival. Typically there is resistance to results that are perceived as a loss of personal choice and control. Resistance is also encountered when others feel they have inadequate information about roles, operations, or exact changes.

You can lessen the resistance by seeking out these concerns, by involving others along the way, and by answering people's questions. Share your plans with them, and be accepting of their input. But always focus on what needs to be accomplished instead of fighting or worrying about the resistance.

AND AGAIN . . .

Let's review the principles of coevaluation, particularly the values inherent in it as *an ongoing process* that is important for your success in bringing the organization to a more effective level. Organizational learning is

- Promoted by organizational leadership in a climate of trust.
- A process that allows people to examine why something succeeded and why something failed without fear of consequences.
- An opportunity for staff to collaborate with others in the organization and with external parties.
- Time and effort well spent, saving money in the long run by making better use of limited resources and bringing results that ensure the organization's health and viability in a changing environment.

The three steps are deceptively simple: ask good questions, collect the right information, share and make decisions with the information you collect. Applied with thought, they lead to effectiveness, empowerment, and excellence. In the next few chapters, we explore their implications at each level of an organization.

References

Fisher, L. R. "Learning and Change: The Desired Outcomes of Evaluation." In S. T. Gray (ed.), *A Vision of Evaluation.* Washington, D.C.: INDEPENDENT SECTOR, 1993.

Senge, P. *The Fifth Discipline.* New York: Doubleday/Currency, 1990.

Stockdill, S. H., and Stoehr, M. *How to Evaluate Foundation Programs.* St. Paul, Minn.: St. Paul Foundation, 1993.

CHAPTER TWO

Empowering Staff for Evaluation

When people ask good questions that apply to their roles as individuals, they gain information that can help them improve their effectiveness. Likewise, when people ask good questions that apply to their roles as part of a staff, both they and their organizations can benefit.

This chapter looks at the process of coevaluation—that is, the process of continuous, constructive, cooperative evaluation introduced in Chapter One—as it involves the paid staff of a nonprofit organization. As individuals, organization staff members often have the opportunity to isolate a concern and make it their focus to solve. They can make a habit of thinking about what is going well and what is going less well, and of being watchful for learning moments. In group settings, they can join others to work to make the organization better through the learnings coevaluation makes possible.

COEVALUATION AND THE LEADER

Coevaluation is easier when the leadership sets the standard and the tone for the agency. Is it impossible without the leadership's support and commitment? No, just much harder. However, the organization's formal leadership must believe in coevaluation and commit its efforts to live it, if the organization is to fully achieve excellence.

Indeed, there are some principles of the new paradigm that only the organization's formal leadership—board and chief executive—can address:

- Only leadership can allow the whole organizational system to be evaluated in a consistent, ongoing manner to achieve internal effectiveness and external results.

- Only leadership can ensure the environment is as risk free as possible so that, while maintaining accountability, success and failure are looked upon equally as opportunities for learning.

- Only leadership can create a climate of trust that permeates the way an organization works. Leaders need to operate from a mind-set that people and process contribute equally to success, that both need nurturing, that both evolve through guided growth. Leaders demonstrate trust by encouraging collaboration, building community inside and outside the organization, promoting individual and group achievements, and sharing organization rewards and accolades.

- Only leadership can ensure that the organization's vision, mission, and values are in agreement and are legitimate property of all constituents of the organization.

- Only leadership can encourage everyone in monitoring the ethical behavior of the total organization.

In effect, without executive leadership embracing the vision of coevaluation, the total system that is the organization will be unable to reach excellence through continuous learning.

This book consciously avoids the concept that leadership is the sole responsibility of the board and executive management. We argue that the process of coevaluation—of ongoing organizational learning—can take place *any*where at *any* time by *any*one in the organization. Leadership, too, is not limited to only a few within the organization. In fact, committing yourself to continuous evaluation is an expression of leadership, wherever your job happens to fall on the organization chart.

As an individual, you can lead others through the coevaluation process by asking good, strategic questions, collecting accurate information, and sharing and using that information to make decisions.

You can also lead by

- Promoting the language and behavior of the new paradigm in all your professional relationships.

- Valuing the giving and receiving of feedback, thus showing others that you accept success and failure as part of learning, not keeping score.

- Encouraging joint decisions and collaborative action plans.

- Demonstrating to others how to use coevaluation tools and techniques to move the organization forward.

- Inviting others inside and outside the organization to join you in being more effective.
- Modeling ethical behavior for others.

These are all leadership characteristics and responsibilities.

COEVALUATION AND THE INDIVIDUAL EMPLOYEE

As an individual—regardless of your job—you can use coevaluation at any time, but a particularly convenient time would be as you plan your work week. Think about your role in the organization, its vision, and how your work contributes to its effectiveness and its mission. We might call it "evaluating at your desk."

Evaluating at your desk demands an emphasis on "I" and "my." Good questions bearing on the vision, mission, values, and ethics of your organization might include

- Vision

  How does my work help communicate the vision of the organization?
- Mission

  How does my work promote or limit the organization's ability to reach its mission?

  How can I help the organization become more effective at what it does?
- Values and Ethics

  How do I convey or not convey the organization's values in my work with other employees or in my interactions with customers and clients?

  Have I helped board members know and understand our bylaws?

  Have I put proper procedures in place for ensuring compliance with all laws that apply to my job?
- Outside Contacts

  What image of the organization do I project in the relationships I have with customers, clients, patrons, volunteers, and the community at large?
- Role

  What is my role in the organization?

  In what ways do I successfully fulfill my role?

  Where would I change? Why?
- Professional Development

  Are there skills I need to become more efficient and effective in my job?

  If so, how do I obtain additional training in these areas?

An Individual Employee Using the Power of Evaluation

Jim is a receptionist in a medium-sized nonprofit organization. His job assignments include greeting clients and assisting them with their needs, greeting community members as they come into the center for service or to attend various meetings, answering the telephone, assisting staff with their word processing, and other duties as assigned. Here's how the effectiveness feedback loop (Figure 1.1) worked for Jim:

1. *Asking good questions.* One Monday morning, Jim took a few minutes before the phone started ringing to think about the week ahead. His organization has a form to help in this process and Jim used it to note things he needed to do. Ever conscious of the organization's vision and mission, he also identified one aspect of his work that he would like to evaluate that week. He asked, "What else do I need to do to help people feel welcomed, cared for, and served effectively?"

Jim chose as his outcome to improve greeting and assisting clients so that his care for them and his concern for their success would be more apparent.

2. *Collecting information.* To collect information, Jim gave the bilingual staff a set of questions to ask clients in their classes: "What happens first when you come to the center?" "What kind of impression do you have when you first arrive?" "What would you like to be different?"

3. *Sharing and using information.* At the end of the week, Jim met with the bilingual staff. He learned that his presence usually made a good impression on clients. Many of them saw him as patient and very willing to answer questions and give assistance. However, clients reported that Jim sometimes signaled nonverbally that he was too busy to take care of them, that other things seemed more important. Jim, the bilingual staff, and the staff supervisor reflected on the information, discussed various factors and ideas, and finally agreed that word processing was getting in the way of client relations. Almost all requests for word processing were reaching Jim early in the workday—exactly when most of the clients were arriving. The group mutually agreed that procedures needed to be changed. No word processing assignments would be made—and no leftover work from the previous day would be expected—between 8 and 9 A.M. Jim's primary responsibility then would be to greet clients and deal with their needs.

Again: At the beginning of the next week, Jim once again took a few minutes to think about the week ahead and identify one aspect of his work that he wanted to learn how to do more effectively.

COEVALUATION AND THE WORK GROUP

The coevaluation process in group settings places the emphasis on "we" and "our." Good questions apply to various facets of the organization:

- Vision and Mission

  What do our vision and mission statements mean to our staff and our clients?

  To what extent is our organization communicating its vision and fulfilling its mission?

  In what ways does the work of our staff contribute to the vision and the mission?

  How can all members of our organization work to help the organization communicate its vision and realize its mission?

- Values and Ethics

  What does our organization value?

  How are organizational values communicated throughout our organization?

  To what extent are our value statements demonstrated in our organization's operating procedures?

  In what ways do staff convey or not convey our organization's values in their work with other employees and customers?

- Organizational Philosophies and Policies

  In what ways are our organizational philosophies and policies communicated throughout the organization?

  To what extent are the philosophies and policies a part of our organization's operating procedures?

  What needs to change to make these philosophies and policies an ongoing part of our organization?

  Do any philosophies and policies get in the way of our organization's success?

  Are we fulfilling all requirements for our legal standing? If not, why not?

  What can we do to make certain they are fulfilled in the future?

- Outside Contacts

  How can staff relationships with customers or clients be characterized?

  In what ways are these relationships strong?

  In what ways could these relationships be improved?

- Volunteerism

  What are the strengths and weaknesses of our volunteer recruitment?

  What are the strengths and weaknesses of our volunteer orientation and training?

  To what extent are we able to retain our good volunteers?

  If they leave, why do they leave?

  Is there something we can do to retain good volunteers for longer periods of time?

  To what extent do we tolerate less effective volunteers? Why?

  What are the strengths and weaknesses of our use of volunteers?

  What do volunteers like about working with our organization? What do they dislike?

- Programs

  In the most ideal situation, how do we define success?

  What does success look like? What does success feel like?

  Who or what will change if program staff are successful?

  What activities help our program staff realize success?

  What activities get in the way of our program staff realizing success?

  How will program staff know when they are successful?

  What factors promote or limit success?

  How can strengths be built upon and weaknesses addressed?

  How will our program staff tell others about success?

  What will our program staff be able to show others that demonstrates success?

- Outcomes

  Who or what is going to change as a result of what we do in this organization?

  How will we know if that change has occurred?

  How can our program activities be modified or changed, if needed, to more readily realize the desired outcomes?

- Activities

  Are our program or organizational activities leading to intended outcomes?

  What are the strengths and weaknesses of our activities?

What needs to change to make them more effective in helping the organization communicate its vision, meet its mission, and reach its outcomes?

- Staff Meetings

Does each department have regular staff meetings?

What does our staff gain from attending these meetings?

What is the value of these meetings?

What would make the meetings more useful to staff?

What would make the meetings more efficient?

When staff gathers—weekly, monthly, and quarterly or in committees, task forces, and teams—you can employ the process of coevaluation. The Questioning Agenda discussed in Chapter One is a powerful tool for use during meetings.

A simpler technique, while not as powerful, can still make a difference. Consider the scenario in Exhibit 2.1.

The scenario in Exhibit 2.2 shows the power of the process of coevaluation in a planning meeting.

AND AGAIN . . .

Coevaluation—cooperative, continuous, constructive evaluation—needs to permeate the whole staff of a nonprofit organization. It prospers best when the top executive and the board adopt it, promote it, and use it in their own activities as well as recommending it to everyone else, but anyone can do it. At any level, from the layout of an office to the launch of a multimillion-dollar fund raising campaign, it helps to

- Ask good questions.
- Collect information.
- Share and use the information you collect to make decisions.

Evaluation at a Work Group Meeting

In this agency the staff identified and repeatedly used two good questions at each weekly meeting.

1. *Asking good questions.* The good questions asked each week were "With what clients are you having difficulty? What can we learn from these cases?"

2. *Collecting information.* The discussion was structured in a way that everyone felt free to admit to having difficulties. They presented information to other staff who helped by reviewing the case, sharing similar experiences, and relating what was done in their cases. This reflection and sharing time enabled the group to jointly explore the learnings and to suggest techniques for handling the case based on those learnings.

3. *Sharing and using information.* At the next staff meeting, individuals with the troublesome clients reported what they tried, if it worked, and what they learned from the experience.

Again: Later in the meeting the good questions were asked again; the ongoing process of coevaluation was working.

Exhibit 2.1. One Use for Coevaluation.

Evaluation at an Annual Planning Meeting

The mission of this nonprofit is "to provide teenagers with opportunities where they can achieve success and feel good about themselves with a focus on respect for self, others, and the environment." Various program offerings are designed to help youth appreciate the environment, develop outdoor living skills, and learn about, interact with, and appreciate other cultures. Once a year the staff and board meet together to plan for the coming period.

1. *Asking good questions.* At a preliminary meeting, the staff and board members identified areas of focus and agreed to use a questioning agenda to plan. One area of focus concerned inner-city teenagers. The outcome chosen was "How successful are we in recruiting and serving inner-city teens?"

2. *Collecting information.* The staff and board agreed that they needed both quantitative and qualitative information to answer the question, learn from the answers, and plan for the next year. A team of selected staff, volunteers, and board members divided up teens currently enrolled in programs and, in face-to-face visits, asked selected questions to discover teens' views. The team also tried to contact teens who were no longer enrolled in programs and get their opinions. In addition, other staff members reviewed files and records of participation over a five-year period and prepared summaries of the number of inner-city teenagers served and of the information in the files that might give an indication of successful or unsuccessful program service. A daylong working session was held using a questioning agenda.

3. *Sharing and using information.* The meeting members learned that the number of inner-city teens in the program increased from 5 percent to 15 percent over the five-year period. While the recruitment level was within their definition of success, learnings from the teens' comments surfaced themes such as irrelevance to their lives, undue pressure from peers, and infrequent follow-up from volunteers. Action plans were designed to address these issues over the next planning period.

Again: The group agreed to meet in six months and determine whether midcourse corrections to the plan were needed; the final review of the action plan would be at the next annual planning meeting.

Exhibit 2.2. Ongoing Evaluation and Annual Planning.

CHAPTER THREE

The Board's Role in Evaluation

A dynamic board is a critical factor in organizational effectiveness. A dynamic board gets involved, is committed, and relates well to the executive director. The board is a nonprofit's top level of governance, legally responsible for the organization—including creating and communicating its vision and determining, reviewing, and carrying out its mission—and for hiring, evaluating, and when necessary replacing the executive director. In the best nonprofits, Knauft and Gray note in *Profiles of Excellence* (1991), the board's role extends beyond these legal and oversight obligations:

- *Board responsibilities:* The board is fully informed about all the workings of the organization, ensuring that programs and activities reflect the vision and effectively carry out the mission. It also remains focused on general policy and approving long-range and annual operating plans and budgets. The board reviews and approves periodic financial reports and appoints independent auditors. In all but very small or emerging groups, the responsibility for day-to-day management is delegated to the executive director. However, it is important to be flexible because the board can be extremely helpful with implementation and the executive director valuable in shaping policy.
- *Board and executive director:* In the best nonprofits, the board and executive director forge a special working relationship, grounded in mutual trust and responsibility, two-way communications, and power sharing.
- *Board membership:* The dynamic board pays close attention to the character and diversity of its membership. It regularly seeks out new blood, not only

as a source of new ideas, but to renew itself and adapt to changing circumstances in ways that help the organization achieve its mission.

• *Involvement in fund raising:* An effective board is actively involved in fund raising. Board members decide when to initiate fund raising and membership campaigns. They identify and call on potential contributors. When appropriate, they make personal financial contributions. The board ensures that adequate financial resources are secured and properly managed.

BOARD-LEVEL COEVALUATION

Board members might reflect on these four categories in terms of the coevaluation processes discussed in Chapters One and Two. Individuals and groups within an organization can engage in their own process of continuous and collaborative evaluation . . . but the support of the board makes a tremendous difference. The risk-free environment, in particular, begins with the board—the board can fire the executive director, and the executive director needs to know that it is safe to deal with a problem constructively rather than bury it or shoot the messenger in the interest of personal job security. That sense of safety cascades across the organization. When the executive director is comfortable about taking a clear-eyed look at capital outlays, someone like Jim— the receptionist introduced in Chapter Two—can feel comfortable about stopping to ask what people really think when they're not complaining about the service.

Effects on the Organization

When the board really backs and uses coevaluation, people across the organization will make thousands of good decisions that the board will never hear of. Nonetheless those decisions will cascade back through the organization and make it ever more effective and more powerful at conveying its vision and carrying out its mission.

• *Influencing the organization.* One important role the board can assume in an ongoing process of evaluation is to be the chief force for the promulgation of organization learning. In addition to modeling coevaluation as a means of making the board itself more effective, the board can promote the technique and encourage others in the organization to use the coevaluation process.

One way to do this is to let staff know that the board expects "why" explanations in staff materials instead of just the "what." The board can request learning reports instead of progress reports. Learning reports would include presentation and analysis of organizational effectiveness on issues of strategic importance along with alternative courses of action for the board's consideration. That is, the board needs to specify reports that include responses to questions such as, What are the nature of the environment and the changing dynamics within which we are working on this initiative? What are the critical issues? What do our members, donors, experts, and other publics think? How is the organization being affected? What is the role of the organization in addressing this issue? Are human and financial resources sufficient and appropriately deployed to carry out the program and operational activities to meet the stated intentions?

Sufficient background information must be provided to enable the board to participate in this dialogue and assessment. Be sure to allocate time for in-depth discussion of how this relates to the vision, mission, and goals of the organization. Emphasis should be on participation and future actions. One or two hours during each meeting is not unreasonable.

Learning reports that engage the board in assessing the effectiveness of the organization in the context of its current environment help the board be more engaged in the process of coevaluation.

The board also needs to look for opportunities to encourage cross-unit collaboration. It should celebrate team achievement when it appears, and should identify and remove any organizational barriers that are getting in the way. In addition, it should work with the executive director to set up organization rewards to recognize excellence wherever it occurs in the system, among both groups and individuals.

- *Board and executive director.* The leadership team quality of the board and executive director relationship can serve as a model for the director and staff relationships as well. Power sharing is a natural by-product of a commitment to organizational learning.

- *Board responsibilities.* The board can stay focused on general policy and long-range goals by asking for regularly scheduled presentations of learnings that address strategic questions.

- *Board membership.* Close attention to the character and diversity of membership can be achieved through the regular use of good questions focused on the adaptive and representational qualities of board members.

- *Involvement in fund raising.* An organization's increased effectiveness through applying ongoing evaluation is powerful evidence to use when board members approach funders, contributors, and prospective members.

Effects on the Board

Coevaluation will be an important tool for the board itself, applied in two ways. It can be incorporated into the board's own activities, for example by using a complete Questioning Agenda like the one proposed in Chapter One at board meetings or by adding probing questions to each agenda. The board's use of coevaluation also displays the board's collective spirit and enthusiasm for evidence from the organization that an ongoing process of evaluation—continued learning—is yielding excellence in communicating the vision and achieving the mission.

Board members individually and collectively should probe organizational effectiveness by asking good questions such as the following, derived from their fundamental areas of responsibility.

- Vision and Mission

  Where are we going?

  How do we define success? How will we know when we are successful?

  To what extent is our definition of success consistent with our vision and mission statements?

  To what extent do board members, staff, and all associated with the organization demonstrate commitment to the vision and belief in the mission?

  To what extent are the vision and the mission kept in focus when there is chaos or when pressure is applied to move into new areas?

  What do our vision and mission statements say to others? What do people think about when they read or hear our vision and mission statements? Is that what we intended? If not, why not? Do our vision and mission statements need revision so that they clearly communicate our intentions?

  Is our mission relevant to today's issues and needs? If not, what revisions must be made?

  What impact would new vision and mission statements have on leadership, staffing, organizational priorities and activities, fund raising, and budgets?

- Board Commitment

  To what extent are members of the board fully committed to this organization?

  To what extent do they commit their time, resources, and talents to its growth and development?

- Board Composition

  What skills, backgrounds, experiences, and expertise are needed for this board to make effective decisions for the organization?

  To what extent are those characteristics present within the current board membership? Where do gaps exist?

  Who is being served by this organization?

  To what extent should the membership of the board reflect the client population? Does the board have representation from those who volunteer their time to the organization?

- Directors' Relationships

  To what extent do the directors communicate effectively?

  Is there trust, mutual respect, sharing of power, sharing of ideas and opinions?

  Do the directors persevere through difficult tasks or discussions?

  Do the directors use consensus building? Do they show the ability to make a decision?

  How do relationships need to be strengthened?

- Relationship Between Board and Executive Director

  To what extent is the relationship between the board and executive director a working relationship, grounded in mutual trust, with shared responsibilities and two-way communication?

  How can strengths be built upon? To what extent do the board and the executive director operate in a way that promotes organizational success?

  In what areas are improvements needed? What causes tension? What needs to change so that board members and the director work as a team?

- Legal Responsibilities

  To what extent do all members of the board fully understand their responsibilities and roles, including their legal responsibilities?

  Are board members fully informed of the legal issues related to serving as a director, such as personal injury and property damage; risks related to libel, slander, false imprisonment, breach of contract, breach of fiduciary duty, conflict of interest, mismanagement of funds, failure of supervision, and imprudent investments?

- Fiduciary Responsibilities

  To what extent are all directors aware of their fiduciary responsibilities?

  Where does the money for this organization come from? How are our sources of funding changing? Why is this organization given money?

  How are the funds given to the organization being used?

  How can board members make sure that funds are used for intended purposes? What mechanisms are in place to ensure that funds are being used for intended purposes? How can board members make sure that funds are not being used by staff or board members for personal gain? How clear are the funding priorities?

- General Responsibilities

  Are board members fully informed about the workings of the organization? Do they understand its bylaws?

Are board members focused on general policy and involved with long-range planning?

Are board members involved, to the extent appropriate, in the management and implementation of the organization's initiatives?

Are directors involved in monitoring the expenditure of funds?

Are directors involved in controlling the direction of the organization?

- Fund Raising Responsibilities

Is the board actively involved in fund raising for the organization?

Do directors take their roles in fund raising seriously enough to be serving on committees as requested and following through with assignments?

Are board members sufficiently involved in fund raising? Does their involvement need to be strengthened or expanded?

- Board Meetings

Are board meetings an effective use of members' time and talents?

Are they held at times and locations that help ensure that members can be present?

Are they conducted in a way that gives the board needed information and enables the board to make decisions?

To what extent do board members come to the meetings prepared to discuss agenda items and make decisions?

SOME SPECIFIC STEPS

Unique opportunities are available for the board and each member to use *and* model coevaluation. The following suggestions are to get you started.

Changing Meeting Agendas

In Chapter One we introduced the concept of a Questioning Agenda as a way of reframing board meetings. An agenda that lists good strategic questions instead of reports or discussion items keeps the focus on the broader issues with which the board needs to deal.

For example, when board members receive reports prior to the meeting, a Questioning Agenda asks questions like: What did you find in the premeeting materials that tells you the organization is using its resources appropriately? Or, What evidence did you see that the executive director and staff are working toward the long-range achievement of goals as well as current objectives?

These kinds of questions require board members to concentrate on connections between the board and the organization, and between the various responsibilities of the board. A financial report needs to be reviewed for its connection to the fund development plan or to priorities in the annual strategic plan, not just as a statement of income, expenses, and reserves.

These kinds of questions also require reflection, sharing of ideas and opinions that stretch board members' thinking. A board trustee who is also an organization volunteer needs to step outside the volunteer perspective to fully appreciate, digest, and comment on how a capital budget request may lead to mission fulfillment.

Reflecting, connecting, sharing, and planning by board members and staff are characteristics of organizational learning at the highest level.

"Before We Adjourn . . ."

A technique that is particularly suitable for board meetings is to evaluate the meeting itself and the board as a body before adjournment. The following scenario suggests one method.

Evaluation at Each Board Meeting

Sue is newly elected to the board of directors of a three-year-old nonprofit organization dedicated to helping adults with mental retardation and brain injury achieve independence and gain self-esteem.

1. *Asking good questions.* Prior to the board meeting, Sue approached the chair and suggested that there might be ways to improve the meetings. The chair agreed and asked her to propose the topic. When she raised it at the meeting, other members concurred. The good question formulated was "What can we do, together and individually, to improve the effectiveness of board meetings?"

2. *Collecting information.* Sue worked with other members and staff to identify a way to collect information to answer the question. The group discovered a questionnaire developed by the American Society of Association Executives that was designed to measure a board's effectiveness as a group at the end of a meeting or at the end of their organization's planning year. Sue and her team adapted the questionnaire to suit the specific needs of the board. It was first used at the February meeting.

3. *Sharing and using information.* The team summarized responses to the questionnaire and sent the summary to the board as an agenda item. During the March meeting, the board analyzed and discussed the summary. Among other issues, the summary showed many board members were individually concerned about news accounts of a pending lawsuit against a nonprofit organization in the

community. Members wanted to know more about the potential for lawsuits against directors and wanted information on legal issues related to serving as a director.

Immediate plans were made to have the organization's retained legal counsel appear at the next meeting and review both director responsibility and the current legal implications of the case. In addition, the executive director was asked to present options for obtaining director and officer insurance.

Again: The board continued to use the questionnaire findings in other ways, and soon decided the tool was so helpful that it would be used at every board meeting.

To try out the technique, use the simple questionnaire in Exhibit 3.1 at one of your upcoming board meetings.

Information gathered from board members using this questionnaire should be summarized by the board chair and executive director, shared with all board members, and used to make decisions to improve the subsequent board meetings. The board's own commitment to excellence in using the coevaluation process for its own development and improvement serves as a model for everyone in the organization.

Another method is to have each member rate several elements of the meeting using an even simpler form like the one in Exhibit 3.2.

This quick evaluation process yields good information for the executive director and board chair to use in planning the next agenda and meeting. The information is also useful to the staff who prepared the background material.

If time is available at the end of a board meeting, good questions to ask periodically are

- Were the issues we dealt with during this meeting of appropriate concern for the board? Why do you think they were? Were not?

- What benefits did we bring to the organization today? Did we further the organization's mission in the context of its vision?

Board Retreats

Board retreats are designed and held for a variety of reasons. Sometimes the directors need to get together without distractions to reexamine their vision and mission statements and organization values. There may be a need for team building among board members, or between the board and staff, or for directed thinking and discussion on a major issue. Long-range planning may have been set aside at regular meetings until it needs immediate and focused attention. Any or all of these factors may make it desirable for the board to get away together for a while. Whatever the reason, board retreats are natural places to continue the coevaluation process. There is great opportunity for learning to occur in the retreat's intense, focused, uninterrupted environment.

Consider using coevaluation to shape the retreat. Focus on a significant issue facing the whole organization—a major capital building plan and funding campaign, perhaps, or a complete system restructuring effort. The following scenario describes one such opportunity.

Board Retreat: Dealing with a Tough Issue

George, the executive director of a municipal zoo, and Mina, head of the zoo board, were charged with designing a two-day retreat for eighteen trustees and senior staff members. After much thought, they decided to use the coevaluation process as the agenda for a retreat to deal with organizational ethics.

1. *Asking good questions.* On the first morning, George and Mina helped the attendees clarify the desired outcome (to ensure ethical fulfillment of the zoo's mission) and to develop good questions: What are the ethical standards we strive for? To what extent are our ethical standards demonstrated in our work as a board? As an institution dedicated to education, research, and conservation?

2. *Collecting information.* Throughout the rest of the day and well into the first evening, mixed groups met and pooled information on four issues: commitment to law and beyond, accountability to the common good and the public, respect for individual worth and dignity, and respect for the earth's biological heritage. The collective "here and now" energy, experience, wisdom, and intellectual resources of the group yielded more than enough information to answer the questions.

3. *Sharing and using information.* A good portion of the second day was spent summarizing, analyzing, and reflecting on the groups' findings. George and Mina's meeting leadership skills were put to the test. As the day went on, however, decisions emerged from the discussions and action steps outlined.

The framework for a Zoo Code of Ethics was developed and an ethics team volunteered to continue work on it. Board committee heads, with the agreement of the senior managers who staffed the committees, decided to build ethics checkpoints into their reports and annual plans. Before ending the meeting, attendees shared their learnings as a way of evaluating the retreat itself.

Again: Having personally experienced the coevaluation process, most attendees felt more confident and more empowered to use the process in their own areas of responsibility.

Board Performance and Meeting Evaluation

Before we adjourn the meeting, please take a moment to evaluate how effectively we functioned as a body during the_____board meeting experience.

Using a scale of 5 (high) to 1 (low), circle your response.

1. Effectiveness of
   overall board meeting   5   4   3   2   1

2. Appropriateness of
   the overall agenda   5   4   3   2   1

   Appropriateness of items   5   4   3   2   1

   Questions encouraged
   evaluative reflection
   and inquiry   5   4   3   2   1

3. The agenda:

   Focused on key policy issues   5   4   3   2   1

   Focused on key strategic areas 5   4   3   2   1

4. Rate each key strategic area with regard to the quality of the board's strategic discussion and outcomes. (A rating of 5 would indicate that we focused on the policy dimension of issues or had a very strong strategic discussion.)

   Strategic areas addressed:

   _____ 5   4   3   2   1

   _____ 5   4   3   2   1

Exhibit 3.1. Meeting Evaluation Questionnaire.

_____ 5   4   3   2   1

_____ 5   4   3   2   1

_____ 5   4   3   2   1

_____ 5   4   3   2   1

5. Rate the quality of the meeting
   facilities and services during
   this meeting.   5   4   3   2   1

6. What is your best suggestion for further improving our board meeting?

_____ 5   4   3   2   1

_____ 5   4   3   2   1

_____ 5   4   3   2   1

GENERAL COMMENTS:

Signature *(optional)*

_____

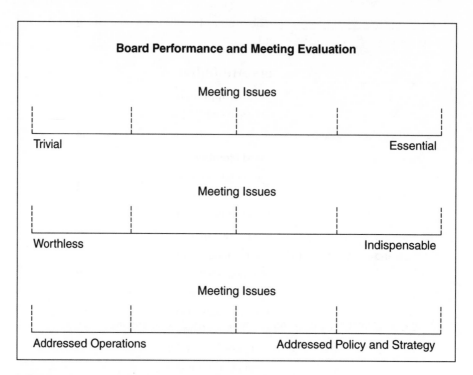

Exhibit 3.2. Quick Index to Meeting Effectiveness.

The Annual Meeting and Report

Annual meetings provide another opportunity to present organizational learn-ings openly and honestly in front of a public audience. Typically each function of the agency presents a report, through either a staff or board representative. The reports tend to be highlighted pieces of the whole, and it is almost always the executive director or board chair who integrates them and pulls together the big picture.

Consider, instead, an annual meeting where the learning and actions derived from coevaluation are reported by teams or joint board-staff work groups. Because coevaluation is ingrained in the operations, collaborative efforts would be highlighted—that is, efforts that crossed traditional functional boundaries. The audience would see and hear the organization's achievement in a new and exciting way.

You can also design an annual report to be a summation of organizational learnings achieved through ongoing coevaluation. When you describe the year's experience and achievements, the document becomes a learning report instead of a retrospective annual statement.

Board Members Are Individuals, Too

A bit of creativity using the coevaluation approach can lead to interesting break-throughs for the organization. The process begins with individuals. The following case sums it up:

Evaluation and the Individual Board Member

Rafael had just finished his first year on the board of an agency that received its funding from a multitude of sources—state and local governments, public and private foundations, individual and corporate contributors.

1. *Asking good questions.* Rafael had listened to the financial reports at each meeting and tried to review the balance sheets carefully. He began to wonder whether he understood the requirements of the funding and how the funds were being used. Categories of expense appeared to be appropriate, but he was not sure. His good evaluation questions: How are the funds given to the organization being used? Are they used for intended purposes? How would I know? What mechanisms are there to ensure appropriate usage? What can the board do to ensure we fully understand our organization's finances?

2. *Collecting information.* Rafael decided to collect information by talking things over with an accountant with nonprofit experience to enlighten him. The issues related to serving as a director, she explained, included appropriate and inappropriate expense allocations, how to "really read" a balance sheet, and what mechanisms are used by effective nonprofits to monitor fund expenditures.

3. *Sharing and using information.* Rafael felt that it was important for other board members to review this information and determine what meaning, if any, it had for the organization. He asked the board chair for time at the next meeting and presented his learnings. Other directors expressed similar uncertainty about fiduciary responsibilities. It was decided that the executive committee would hold a working session where the board would review the financial policies and practices, and would identify whether additional safeguards were needed to ensure the organization's financial integrity.

Again: Rafael's actions encouraged other board members to think about their roles and to identify ways they, as individuals, could improve board and agency effectiveness. Individuals began asking themselves, "Did I avoid conflict or cause conflict?" "Do I know when I shouldn't bend?"

AND AGAIN . . .

Ideally, coevaluation begins with the board. Only the board can make the environment risk free for the whole organization, including the executive director, and the board itself can multiply its own resources by asking good questions, collecting information, and sharing and using the results. At every turn, in its meetings, retreats, and individual projects, and in the reports and research it requests from the organization, the board is in the best position to make coevaluation work. It can happen without the board—but an organization working at cross-purposes with its board is never going to achieve the heights of effectiveness, empowerment, and excellence of one that enjoys unanimity of spirit.

Reference

Knauft, E. B., and Gray, S. T. *Profiles of Excellence: Achieving Success in the Nonprofit Sector.* Washington, D.C.: INDEPENDENT SECTOR, 1991.

CHAPTER FOUR

How Volunteers Can Contribute to Evaluation

Volunteers are critical partners in an organization's pursuit of excellence. Their unique perspectives bring invaluable information to the natural and ongoing process of organizational learning. For coevaluation—the continuous, constructive, and cooperative process of evaluation integrated into the life of an organization—to succeed, it must involve the volunteers as well as the paid staff. Volunteers must be among those who expect and are expected to gather information through good questions, share the answers, explore the responses, and contribute to the resulting decisions.

Chapters Two and Three discuss how staff and board members should apply coevaluation in their everyday working life. This chapter focuses on how volunteers can also contribute to making an organization effective by using the coevaluation process.

VOLUNTEERING COEVALUATION

Volunteers are part of an organization, involved and outside at the same time, serving but not salaried. The result is a unique way of looking at the organization, with a unique set of experiences and realities. Volunteers are able to ask the good questions from viewpoints different from those of other stakeholders. This special element brought by volunteers—a clearer eye—serves as a particularly valuable complement to the collaborative effort of making the organization better.

Consider how Joel helped his organization because, from his perspective, things weren't working right:

Retaining Volunteers

Joel is a volunteer for a food shelf at a local community center.

1. *Asking good questions.* Joel had worked at the center for a month when he decided that something was wrong. Although ten volunteers were scheduled to work each night, most of the time only two or three actually came. He knew the missing volunteers were committed to the work and so he was puzzled. His good question was "Why are volunteers not coming to the center to help with this program?"

2. *Collecting information.* Joel went to Yvette, the program director, and asked what she thought of the situation. Yvette expressed similar frustration. She said it bothered her, too, but she did not know for sure why it was happening. The work was getting done, so she had not investigated further. After talking it over, they decided it would be a good idea to call the volunteers and say something along the lines of "Volunteer participation at the food shelf has dropped off considerably. Why do you think this is happening?" They thought it best for Joel to do the phone interviews because he was not on staff and because he was also a volunteer. Although the volunteers were hesitant to talk at first, Joel assured them that the staff valued their opinions and would use them only to help the program. He learned that the volunteers, mostly senior citizens and female, were afraid to come to the center at night. The parking lot was poorly lit and recent newspaper articles about increasing crime in the area worried them.

3. *Sharing and using information.* Joel and Yvette reviewed this information, reflected on it, and decided that the hours for stocking the food shelves could easily be changed so that volunteers could leave earlier. They also shared their learnings and plans with the community center director. He eagerly picked up on the results, agreed to look at the parking lot situation, and volunteered to contact the police district's community representative.

Again: The center director found the information very useful in getting a board appropriation for new lighting, and for talking with the police. He decided to use the coevaluation process to determine if clients in all center programs shared the volunteer concerns and had more ideas to improve security.

To take full advantage of its volunteers' experience and insight, an organization needs to reach out and make it clear that participation at that level is welcome. In Joel's community center, scores of volunteers and their supervisor had noted the existence of a problem, but "the work was getting done" and all the people involved dismissed the difficulty as an unpleasant and unavoidable aspect of the center's valuable work. When Joel addressed it instead of dismissing it, several helpful measures immediately surfaced—some even without cost to the organization. Yvette reacted very well to Joel's proposal and some real coevaluation got done, and that is very much to her credit—many a supervisor would have said or implied that it was Joel's job to stock shelves and her job to manage the workforce, and the idea would have died on the spot. Nonetheless, the center could and should have done much more. Volunteer orientation materials and briefings should have emphasized the center's need for volunteers' minds as well as their hands, and invited them to look for potential improvements in service and structure. In her contacts with her volunteers, Yvette should have found time to talk about how things were going, and to ask what was going well or badly for them. When the center director decided to spread the coevaluation process to clients in other center programs, he should have expanded its emphasis to volunteers as well—rather than assuming that volunteers would spontaneously engage in coevaluation on their own just because Joel had done so.

Volunteers also have the advantage of interacting and establishing relationships with staff, clients, and directors alike. Freely crossing organization boundaries as they go about their work, they sometimes have greater contact with those served by the organization than many staff members. Consider, for example, the differing experience of a docent at a public museum, who sees and talks with hundreds of museum guests throughout the year, and that of the museum director, who may see no one but museum staff and major donors.

Similarly, volunteers often serve on the board of directors and thus bring their unique perspective to still another set of organizational learning partners. In the following scenario, notice how Julie helped the board of directors reflect on its community representation:

Diversifying Board Membership

Julie was a volunteer for six years for an organization with a mission "to serve the community directly and indirectly through culturally based programs." The organization provides emergency assistance and nonjudgmental support systems for individuals and their immediate and extended families, and programs designed to foster and encourage self-direction and self-determination.
Recently Julie was asked to serve on the board of directors.

1. *Asking good questions.* During a board meeting, Julie and other committee members reviewed service statistics. Julie asked good questions: "Do we know who our clients are? How about the board, do we reflect our client population?"

2. *Collecting information.* Staff were asked to review client data and present statistics at the next board meeting. The staff developed a client profile showing gender, ethnic background, and socioeconomic status.

3. *Sharing and using information.* The board members reviewed the data and concluded that the board needed better representation of community leaders and clients living in the neighborhood. The membership subcommittee was asked to identify a slate of potential members through a program of outreach and community communications.

Again: Prompted by Julie's effort, the board adopted a policy of requiring its nominating committee to review board representativeness as part of its annual process.

Unique perspectives, broad relationships, and day-to-day interactions with staff and clients should help volunteers ask good questions, collect information, and use the results collaboratively with others to improve the organization. When coevaluation is part of the culture, the volunteers are empowered and the organization rises to a new level.

SOME SPECIFIC STEPS

Some of the techniques described in Chapters One through Three can be adapted to the volunteer role. Review these chapters to trigger ideas. Here are some refreshers to get you started:

• *Formal meetings.* Meetings are natural opportunities to practice coevaluation. Volunteers often meet with staff on a formal basis to report on activities, review procedures, or keep up to date on organization developments. You— whether you're a volunteer or a staff member—can encourage the use of a Questioning Agenda at these regular meetings. (See Chapter One.) Or, as a participant, model the process by asking good questions such as What is working well among the volunteers? What isn't?

• *Casual conversation.* Volunteers meet informally over coffee or while on duty, and these small gatherings often identify issues or suggestions to make the organization more effective. Almost equally often, those solutions die as they're born. An organization that engages everyone in coevaluation encourages people to stay awake—to tune in even to passing comments that reveal insight into things that could improve, and to think through how to turn those comments into action and brainstorm ways to share the information with others in the organization. Volunteers like Joel and Julie can do this on their own, of course. It sometimes takes an unreasonable amount of patience and persistence on their part to get the message across, but it multiplies their value and contribution manyfold when they have the energy to do so. On the other hand, an organization that reaches out to its volunteers and makes it easy for them to share their expert opinion on whatever it is they do will find it has many more Joels and Julies in hand, and many more good ideas that leverage its resources and improve its service.

- *Retreats and conventions.* It is very effective to hold an annual meeting for volunteers to report on their successes—and failures—from the learning perspective. An organization needs to give people a chance to say to each other, "Here's what we did, why and how. Here's what we as volunteers learned and will do in the future." When you take away the pressure of day-to-day responsibilities for a while and encourage people to share their insight, ideas multiply.

- *Newsletters.* Often organizations have a publication or newsletter designed especially for volunteers. The organization should encourage the editor to provide continuous learning material about the coevaluation process and to promote coevaluation activities among the volunteers. Anyone with ideas, good questions, or articles should be welcome to submit them.

- *Staff interaction.* Staff should provide volunteers with continuing development activities about the techniques of good questioning, collecting information, sharing information, and making decisions. An organization should encourage the use of these training activities as a forum for the exchange of expertise among volunteers. The backgrounds and experiences of volunteers are varied, and the expertise brought to the organization by volunteers has great potential for building the organization's capacity to learn.

- *Community and professional activity.* Rather than hoarding its volunteers, an organization should encourage them to take part in other volunteer groups or networks. The coevaluation process improves exponentially as it spreads and as people share the evidence of its impact.

STARTER QUESTIONS

Anyone can act as a champion of the coevaluation process. A good start is to make sure you are thoroughly knowledgeable about coevaluation and the techniques discussed in this book. Here are some good questions tailored to volunteers:

- Vision and Mission
  Do I understand the organization's vision and mission?

How does my work promote or limit the organization's ability to reach its mission?

What can I do to help the organization be more successful in communicating its vision and reaching its mission?

- Values and Ethics

What are the shared values of this organization?

What ethical choices do I make as part of my role as a volunteer?

What is the organization's code of ethics?

Are the choices I make in line with the organization's values and code of ethics? If not, what do I need to do to make sure that the choices I make are in line?

- Outside Contacts

What image of the organization do I project in the relationships I have with staff, customers, clients, patrons, other volunteers, and the community at large?

In what ways are these relationships strong? In what ways could these relationships be improved?

- Role

What is my role in the organization?

In what ways do I successfully fulfill my role?

Where could I change? Are there skills I need to work on to become more efficient and effective in my role as a volunteer?

- Volunteerism

What are the strengths and weaknesses of the organization's volunteer recruitment?

What are the strengths and weaknesses of volunteer orientation and training?

What are the strengths and weaknesses of the ways the organization uses volunteers?

If volunteers are leaving, why do they leave?

- Outcomes

How does my work as a volunteer help the organization reach its goals?

What can I do to help the organization be more successful in achieving the outcomes it aims for?

- Activities

Is what I do as a volunteer leading to intended outcomes? What are the strengths and weaknesses of my work? What can I do to help the organization be more successful in its work with clients?

Here's another example of a volunteer using the coevaluation process—beginning with good questions—to help her organization.

Needing Additional Support

Lynn became a volunteer for a domestic abuse program. Her role was to answer calls from women who had been abused and to help them as needed. Her help might include finding a temporary shelter, providing a referral to a counselor, being there to talk, or helping a woman think through her options and next steps.

1. *Asking good questions.* After her first three weeks, Lynn had worked with nine cases and was beginning to feel frustrated in her role as volunteer. Although she had participated in a six-week intensive training program, Lynn now had many questions. She wanted to talk about her feelings and how she was handling cases. Her good question became "Do other volunteers feel the need for additional support?"

2. *Collecting information.* Lynn called the other volunteers who had gone through training with her and found they had similar questions. She summarized her notes and decided to talk with the volunteer coordinator.

3. *Sharing and using information:* Lynn met with the volunteer coordinator and reported that a number of volunteers would value monthly meetings to talk about their experiences. She suggested forming a buddy system where one volunteer could call another to help deal with the stress. The volunteer coordinator was excited about the information and the suggestions but lacked the time to put a program together. Lynn said she would be willing to plan the first meeting and suggested that at that meeting volunteers should consider how they might assume responsibility for scheduling monthly meetings and developing a buddy system. The volunteers met and worked out plan both for monthly meetings and for developing the buddy system.

Again: The volunteers decided to spend some time at each monthly meeting reviewing the organization's vision and mission and asking questions about their role in communicating the vision and achieving the mission.

AND AGAIN . . .

Everyone's ideas have value—and everyone has ideas. Unfortunately, many organizations act as though having ideas is the province of people with particular jobs, and people in other jobs just carry out ideas. By contrast, coevaluation—

continuous, cooperative, constructive evaluation—starts from the premise that organizational adaptability or change is *everybody's* job. Volunteers can be particularly useful in the coevaluation process because their unique half-outside position may let them see more clearly than organizational old-timers, without assumptions about what can and can't be done. A volunteer who wants something to change can use the coevaluation process whether or not the organization as a whole has adopted it—though it's much easier when it is part of the culture—to enlist others to help, develop and share information, and make both the individuals and the organization more effective in communicating their vision and carrying out their mission.

CHAPTER FIVE

Using Client Feedback to Improve Programs and Services

All too often, nonprofit agencies operate on what Steve Mayer (1993) calls the "deficits model"—the idea that distressed people and communities are defined by what they need: their problems, handicaps, and pathologies. Agency staff, in this view, are the ones who fill the deficits—solve the problems, provide adaptations for the handicaps, treat the pathologies—while clients simply accept the services provided by those who know what to do.

But coevaluation—continuous, cooperative, constructive evaluation—really is *everybody's* job. To produce maximum benefit in terms of effectiveness, empowerment, and excellence, coevaluation can't stop at the borders of the organization chart; it must go out into the stakeholder community and engage participants and clients. The people an organization serves, in the final analysis, are the ones who matter. They know better than anyone how well or badly things are going, and they can play a vital role in helping an organization improve the programs and services it provides.

CLIENTS AND COEVALUATION

The deficits model discards a great deal of human potential. In practice, people always have strength and insight they could bring to bear, though they may react passively in systems that encourage or require them to do so. An organization that makes coevaluation a way of life seeks and welcomes its constituents' judgments on the quality of its services; it recognizes that it needs to know how effective those services are in practice, and how efficiently they are provided.

An organization that encourages its clients to share feedback with service providers will help improve its performance, and it will help its clients reach their own goals and meet their own needs—both in relation to the vision and the immediate mission and in terms of overall self-efficacy. Few things in life are so empowering as the experience of changing the course of an organization that has power to affect your well-being. At every turn, in written materials, spoken messages, and nonverbal communications, staff and volunteers should assure participants and clients that their satisfaction and success is the organization's success. The feedback participants and clients provide is not idle complaining or self-serving praise; it helps the organization achieve its mission of service in the context of its vision.

SOME SPECIFIC STEPS

It is simple to adapt the processes of coevaluation to the client community. The basic essential is to make it clear that the organization expects to learn from its clients as well as teach and help them, and that it genuinely wants to improve the effectiveness and quality of its program and services.

As outlined in Chapter One, the keys to the process are to ask good questions, get the information that answers the questions, and then share and use the information to make improvements. It can be useful for clients to read that material—and the rest of this book—for themselves, but staff and volunteers who see clients as resources rather than targets can release the power of coevaluation in the client community whether or not anyone there ever sees this book. The following scenario shows how one client, by using the steps, improved the training she was receiving.

The Aware Client

For eighteen months, Ginger had been a client at a center that used computers to help clients learn various subjects. Ginger liked the computers the center was using when she started there. However, the center recently purchased new equipment. All of a sudden, the teaching routines were timed and Ginger became very frustrated. If she spent too much time on a problem, the computer moved on to the next problem and did not let her finish.

1. *Asking good questions.* Ginger wondered if other clients were also having trouble. Her good question became "What are other clients' reactions to the new computers?"

2. *Collecting information.* During the break in a session, Ginger asked other students about their experiences with the new computers. She found that nine of the twelve were having difficulty.

3. *Sharing and using information.* Ginger and her classmates approached the computer teacher to talk about their problems. The teacher listened to their concerns and thanked them for the information. She was not aware that the new computers were causing so much trouble. She checked the program setup and found that the timing function was optional. Since it clearly wasn't helping the students, she turned it off.

Again: Ginger and her classmates found that asking good questions, collecting information, and sharing information could help make the center a better place. They continued to go through these steps when issues arose.

Good Questions Are the Key

Client feedback can help an organization with overall performance, not just with specific services such as the training discussed in the scenario. Here are some sample questions like the ones in previous chapters, adapted to the client perspective. An agency that wants to know how well it is doing in every respect will share such questions with its clients—and listen very carefully indeed to their response.

- Vision

  Why does this organization exist?

  How can I help communication its vision?

- Mission

  What do I see as the real purpose of this organization—its mission?

  How can I help it carry out that mission?

- Values

  What does this organization value?

  How do board members, staff members, or volunteers display the organization's values as they work with me?

  What do they need to do to better show me that they value me as a client?

- Relationships

  What image of the organization do staff, volunteers, and board members project when they meet with me or see me?

  In what ways are my relationships with staff, volunteers, and board members strong?

In what ways could these relationships be improved?

- Quality of Service

  What do I like about this organization?

  How can these areas be strengthened?

  What do I not like about this organization?

  What can be done to reduce these problems?

  What can staff, volunteers, or board members do to make this organization better?

Gathering Information

As with other coevaluation participants, it isn't enough for clients to ask good questions of themselves and their fellows. The important next step is get solid information to help answer them. Some clients will already understand how to do this; others will need help and encouragement.

For example, suppose a client has a child in a day care program where there is no adequate public transportation. The client raises the question of how the staff and parents could collaborate in providing transportation.

The information-gathering phase could start with development of a short list of options: bus rental, car pooling, chaperoned walks to and from the facility, and so on. The client could make up a written questionnaire with the options listed and ask the other parents about their preferences. Or use the list to talk to other parents individually. Or ask for a group meeting to go over the list, inviting other options.

Chapter One goes into data-gathering options in more detail. It can serve as a source of ideas for clients who know what they want to find out but ask for advice on how to get the information.

Share and Use the Information

Good information is powerful, but only when it is used. Some clients will readily summarize the information they have gathered from their questioning and share it with those who provided it and those who need to make decisions. Others will welcome advice in this area—as will some staff members and volunteers. An organization that integrates coevaluation into its culture will soon develop its own anecdotes and role models for the use of information.

Here's another example of a client providing information that was of great benefit to an organization:

Ongoing Feedback

Thao came to the Anderson Center to learn carpentry, leadership, citizenship, and vocational skills. After participating for six months, he was elected to the Anderson board of directors by his peers.

1. *Asking good questions.* At one meeting, board members asked Thao, "What do other participants like about the center? What don't they like?" Thao answered these questions based on his personal experience. He told the board that he felt uncomfortable answering for other participants.

2. *Collecting information.* Thao and the board decided to develop a brief questionnaire to get feedback from other participants. The questionnaire asked: "Why did you come to the center? How satisfied are you with it? What do you like about it? What would you like to be different?"

All participants completed the questionnaire at one of their citizenship classes. Thao and a subcommittee from the board summarized the information.

3. *Sharing and using information.* Thao and the board learned that the participants were generally satisfied with the program. One area of concern was the citizenship component, however, which did not seem relevant to participants' everyday lives. Program staff were surprised by this and began to ask participants how that might change. Students suggested that there be field trips to attend city council meetings, public hearings, and neighborhood meetings. They also wanted to meet with elected officials.

Again: Thao, the board, and staff found the information obtained from participants to be very useful and decided to repeat the process every six months.

Another way clients can help the organization with evaluation is by serving on an advisory committee or on the organization's board. In those roles, they can help the organization become more effective for themselves and other clients. Consider how Lavette helped her organization:

Concerned Clients

Lavette came to the center to work on her G.E.D. The center had just received funding to build a new facility. Center staff believed that it was important to involve clients in all aspects of center operation and asked Lavette to serve on an advisory committee.

1. *Asking good questions.* An agenda item for one meeting was to choose a name for the new center. It appeared that the staff had already decided on the "HIJ Adult Literacy Center." Lavette had concerns. She personally found the term *literacy* offensive because it conveyed the impression that clients were lacking something. She also thought that it might discourage recruitment. She raised these concerns with other members of the advisory committee and said she thought that other clients, volunteers, and staff should be involved in choosing the name. The good evaluation questions became "What is your reaction to calling the new center the HIJ Adult Literacy Center" and "What other suggestions do you have for the center's name?"

2. *Collecting information.* It was decided that each committee member would collect information by conducting group interviews. Lavette worked with a center volunteer, Malinda, to convene three groups of students to talk about the center's name. Lavette and Malinda conferred after each interview and wrote a one-page summary of what they heard. Copies of their summaries were given to all members of the committee.

3. *Sharing and using information.* The advisory committee reviewed the information. Many people did not like the proposed name. Many wanted a name that emphasized the positive aspects of returning to school to learn skills. A common idea was to emphasize the idea of lifelong learning. The committee decided to propose a new name, the Lifelong Learning Center.

Again: Committee members continued to use the process of evaluation to improve organizational effectiveness in other areas, such as a timely and efficient enrollment process, quality day care, and support and study groups.

AND AGAIN . . .

Especially in times of declining funding and increasing need, no organization can afford to discard resources by defining them out of existence. Nonprofits need to set aside the deficits model and focus on the strengths and potentials of their constituencies. It is vital to encourage participants and clients to share their thoughts and ideas about the program with the organization staff. As people actively look for opportunities to improve the work of the organization and its services, their experience with the coevaluation process will enhance their ability to help themselves and their capacity to help others in all aspects of their lives.

Reference

Mayer, S. E. "Common Barriers to Effectiveness in the Independent Sector." In S. T. Gray (ed.), *A Vision of Evaluation.* Washington, D.C.: INDEPENDENT SECTOR, 1993.

PART TWO

USING ONGOING EVALUATION TO STRENGTHEN KEY AREAS

The basics of coevaluation are very simple—ask good questions, gather information, and share and use the results—but as with most simple truths, the ramifications are rich and complex. The chapters in this section all expand on the theme of finding the right questions, but they apply it in very different aspects of organizational life. None of them use the new term *coevaluation*, but that is what they are all talking about: continuous, cooperative, constructive evaluation that makes a real difference in the quality of life within an organization and in the quality of the services it provides. Many of them take a more scholarly approach than the chapters in Part One, but they will reward even the reader most interested in direct action with useful insights.

In Chapter Six, Astrid Merget and Edward Weaver contrast coevaluation—calling it the new approach to evaluation or ongoing evaluation—with traditional report-card-style evaluation techniques derived from research in the physical sciences. They go beyond what coevaluation is to why it works, and provide a thoughtful discussion of why it can be difficult to implement in nonprofit organizations. Their discussion of the leadership style and structure required to make ongoing evaluation a reality will be particularly helpful to board members and executive directors seeking to make coevaluation a part of the culture of their own organizations.

Chapter Seven, by John Seeley, discusses evaluation as an ongoing learning process in the context of any specific program. It identifies six key elements of program effectiveness and offers questions related to each, and draws a useful distinction among the outputs, outcomes, and impacts of a program. These insights will make it easier for those involved with a program to involve stakeholders in the evaluation process and to produce information that will have a beneficial effect on program performance.

In Chapter Eight, Dennis Young and Humphrey Doermann suggest a wide range of good questions designed to bring coevaluation—that is, continuous evaluation and improvement—to the management of human resources. The authors define human resources as a form of capital, and point out that this human capital is the most important asset of most nonprofits. They highlight similarities and differences between paid staff and volunteers, opening the way to constructive and adaptive management of human resources so as to preserve and develop human capital at the individual, team, and organization-wide level.

Coevaluation depends on information, and Ricardo Millett and Mark Lelle take up the question of information management in Chapter Nine. They introduce the liberating concept that management information systems do not require computers—and that advanced computers do not necessarily produce good management information systems. The key is to concentrate on the use to which information will be put, and to allow the stakeholders' needs rather than the available technology to drive the design of a system. Aimed equally at those who have immersed themselves in information management in the past and those who have avoided the subject, this chapter lays out the real advantages of information management and dispels several myths about it.

Chapter Ten, by Peter Buchanan and Theodore Hurwitz, goes behind the scenes on resource development to show how evaluation can enhance an organization's fund raising efforts over the long term. Of most interest to resource development officers and organization top management and board members, the chapter discusses the importance of measuring the process as well as the results of resource development. It discusses the need to budget enough on resource development even in times when "do more with less" is the watchword, and describes ways to adapt business process management principles to nonprofit fund raising.

In Chapter Eleven, Judy Belk and Michael Daigneault take up the difficult issue of organizational ethics. Contrary to comfortable assumptions about ethical people doing ethical things in good causes, they point out, the real and persistent question for nonprofits is what makes good people make *bad* choices—and what an organization can do to minimize that pressure and encourage ethical behavior at all levels.

Chapter Twelve, by Rebecca Adamson and Edward Weaver, shows how coevaluation can be adapted to the needs of a specific organization. The authors begin by discussing the nature of organizational culture as defined in the scholarly literature, then they present a detailed case study of one organization—the

First Nations Development Institute—that developed an ongoing evaluation process attuned to Native American culture both for its own operations and for those of its grant-making and technical assistance project. The specific process is interesting in itself, and the issues it raises will suggest good questions for the development of coevaluation procedures tailored to other cultures.

In Chapter Thirteen, Patricia Patrizi and James Sanders return to the basic concept that coevaluation is everybody's business and that all organization stakeholders need to see themselves as evaluators—and then explore the role of the outside evaluator in an organization that follows the philosophy outlined in this book. They describe five ways that an outside evaluator can contribute without taking over the reins, and they provide detailed advice on selecting an outside consultant to assist with ongoing evaluation.

CHAPTER SIX

Organizational Behavior and Policy

Astrid E. Merget
Edward T. Weaver

The new approach to evaluation outlined in this volume presupposes new modes of thinking and organizing within nonprofit entities. This chapter sketches out many ways in which the approach breaks with conventions of the past. The first part examines the new thinking that must infuse evaluation for it to be useful and palatable for a nonprofit organization. At the root of our argument is the proposition that the "one best way" of the scientific model must give way to a multiplicity of approaches to doing evaluation. For new thinking to thrive, the organization itself may have to change. Hence the second section of the chapter discusses the organizational imperatives behind the new approach and the tough tasks involved in its implementation.

NEW MODES OF THINKING

While the new view of ongoing evaluation may appear to reject conventional practices, those practices cannot be discarded outright. Rather, many tools are essential if evaluation is to stimulate learning, change, and ultimately effectiveness. The old report-card-style evaluations continue to have value, even though we now need to focus on ways to apply evaluation from the beginning

Portions of this chapter are based on an earlier work by the authors, "Roadmap to Effectiveness: Evaluation" (Gray, 1993).

of an initiative—and continuously thereafter—to take advantage of the opportunity for real-time learning and adaptation and increase the probability of effectiveness in the long run.

This perspective calls for everyone in an organization to develop as evaluative thinkers. It is not enough to relegate such thinking to a professional cadre of evaluators. Evaluation must be embraced as an integral part of the organization's processes, not as an add-on. Success with this approach depends on a relatively risk-free environment, one that rewards openness, learning, adjustment, and change.

Ongoing evaluation, therefore, focuses on organizational and program improvement and their eventual effectiveness. Evaluation for any other purpose has very limited potential for influencing organizational behavior and policy.

Beyond the Report Card

Organizational effectiveness, it is generally agreed, is measured by the extent to which mission and related objectives are achieved as a result of the organization's actions. The ultimate desired outcome of organizational effectiveness, in the nonprofit and philanthropic sectors in particular, is positive impact on people served. Service impact is the real bottom line for nonprofit organizations.

The conventional method of determining service impact—as well as financial accountability—has been this process called evaluation. Evaluation was often strongly influenced by, even patterned after, research designs and methods appropriated from the physical sciences without regard to the requirements of the problem at hand. Taylor and Sumariwalla state the results in formal though discouraging terms: "Approaches grounded in hard sciences and complex quantitative formulations have not proved successful in evaluating human health and development endeavors" (1992, p. 97).

Of course, rigorous research designs—including careful attention to sampling, reliability, and validity of data, and appropriate statistical analysis—have enhanced the base of knowledge that informs the work of nonprofit organizations. *Summative* evaluations, that is, detailed before-and-after testing to calculate change over time, remain important; they contribute after the fact to our knowledge of what happened in the course of a project. But in many if not most human endeavors, the objectives and the program design at the outset of an initiative will change and will not be the same at the end, or at the point of measurement for research or evaluation purposes. This is only one of the realities that complicates the conventional evaluation process. These organizations, programs, and human systems are after all dynamic and not static.

Evaluation as Learning

Given the complexity of organizations and programs that work to bring about change in the human sphere, the traditions of scientific research need supplement. Methods and processes more aligned with the dynamic nature of the entity being evaluated are essential. Approaches that assume that subjects or processes studied are more stable and predictable than is the case in human systems will generally have limited value in influencing organizational behavior and have limited value in propelling organizational effectiveness. Approaches of the past are easy to discount as mere historical information, not a fair view of current practice. Potential users repudiate the results as flawed because the evaluator did not grasp the dynamic nature of the environment. An evaluation that traces the historical record of past impact without discussing the constellation of conditions that made the organization or program effective is of little use.

The conventional approach produces a report card on a program, delivered after the program—or at least the review period—is over. There is no opportunity for the information in the report card to influence behavior during the process and in turn alter the outcome. As a result, evaluation—as practiced in the past—has added little of value to funders, oversight organizations, or organizations that are the subject of evaluation. The focus on past performance has had little impact on current and future effectiveness.

Evaluation of programs and organizations should lead to learning. Evaluation should help address important questions. The answers should tell us "how we're doing" and "what works and what doesn't" as well as "how many were served" and "with what result." Such learning includes knowledge about what factors in the organization's performance brought about particular results. This kind of learning enables the organization to make changes that will foster results more closely matched to its mission and objectives. Learning can empower the organization for future success.

Service impact is influenced by complicated sets of actions and processes that aim at attaining the planned-for result. The operative question in the new approach to evaluation has two parts. First, is the planned result being achieved? and second, what factors in the organization's actions or processes influence the outcome and in what way? The focus is on what is happening now and what effect that is having on the realization of anticipated outcomes. Equally important, feedback must be as near in time to the observation and data collection as possible. The passage of weeks or months—as in conventional evaluation—will significantly diminish the usefulness of the information.

Evaluation must be a process of continuous learning, from the first day of an initiative to the last. Only then can actions and processes adapt so as to realize optimum results. The leverage point for bringing about positive outcomes is not a single one but a combination: the underlying theory and design of the initiative, coupled with the operation of the program and its organization, all shape outcomes. Unless there is learning about what works and how, there is minimal hope for better outcomes in the future. Adaptation—to improve our methods and processes—based on learning through evaluation is the best hope for ensuring organizational effectiveness.

Presumably everyone—or every organization—aspires to be effective. We assert that the right kind of evaluation contributes to organizational effectiveness. Yet the mere mention of evaluation evokes strong feelings, largely negative, from nonprofit and philanthropic professionals. The term conjures up memories of experiences that were little more than hoop jumping and bean counting to satisfy financial accountability and audit requirements of the funders or other external overseers. Most regarded that kind of evaluation as not adding any significant value to a program or organization. The term also engenders feelings of fear that inhibit total honesty. And even funders—United Ways, foundations, governments, and the like—are frequently less than satisfied with formalistic, stylized evaluations; they question how meaningful they are in depicting reality. Most believe grant givers and grant seekers should know how the project is doing, that organizations and programs should be effective, and that funded programs should attain their stated objectives. The reality is that few believe evaluation, as we have known it, yields meaningful answers.

The confusion, frustration, and dissatisfaction with conventional evaluation is not without explanation. As noted earlier, the physical-sciences approach to evaluation, while sometimes useful, rarely matches our real experiences in social or human systems.

There are several difficulties in evaluating programs whose outcome envisions behavioral change in human persons, systems, or communities. First, there is the issue of the number and interrelationship of variables that influence progress toward outcomes. Experiments in the physical sciences work best when they can be limited to one possible cause and a limited range of observable effects, and human systems always involve far more factors than the researcher can monitor. Further, initiatives may take a long time before observable results are apparent—far longer than experiments in the physical sciences customarily run. Many of the conditions to be changed by the programs in human services have evolved in the lives of people, communities, and systems over many years. Changing dysfunctional conditions requires investments of long duration even with the most effective and successful interventions known to work. Expecting dramatic—or even small but measurable—results in the course of a one-to-two-year intervention is often unrealistic. Then there is the challenge of resources to do evaluations. Time, expertise, and funding are necessary. Is it realistic to commit several hundred thousand dollars in a program intervention and budget only $5,000 for evaluation? And often the evaluation is scheduled only at the end of the project—too late to affect the outcome.

During the past decade or so a new and emerging field of study has focused on issues of complexity. Scientists from many disciplines are working together to comprehend convoluted physical and social systems. This is a departure from the traditional approach of disaggregating complex matters in an effort to understand them. These new scientists assert that parts can only be understood in relation to wholes; therefore, they question the reductionist approach to understanding intricate systems. Many of their insights seem to fit better with the everyday reality we experience as professionals and volunteers (Waldrop, 1992). One way to express the shift suggested by the new approach to evaluation is to refocus the interest in *proving* something to *learning and improving* something.

The normative premise behind evaluation is effectiveness in fulfillment of the mission, objective, or purpose of the intervention. For an organization to gauge whether its programs and operations are attaining goals and objectives consistent with its mission means that its leaders and others engaged in the enterprise must be continually learning about the organization. Unfortunately, however, the word *evaluation* resurrects past practices and dissuades many. Making the case for the new approach to ongoing, cooperative evaluation depends on recasting the endeavor as "organizational learning." As a continuous process that contributes to development, it is constantly on the organization's agenda, not an intrusive and episodic event. Making a compelling case also means clarity about the basic reason for engaging in organizational learning. The motive must be rooted in the value of managing effectively to mission.

Absent the norm of effectiveness, evaluation has little purpose. With effectiveness as the impetus, evaluation has meaning. In short, the new approach to evaluation begins with the goal of effectiveness as the unifying principle.

Elements of Ongoing Evaluation

Predicated on the norm of effectiveness, the new approach has many elements that divorce it from the old paradigm. It entails a developmental process, not a report card. It encompasses both internal operations and external results. It is an ongoing process, not episodic and intrusive. It is a collaborative process within the organization and with external parties such as donors and clients or customers. It is a nearly risk-free process, designed for discovery and enlightenment, not a high-stakes process designed for judgment. Judgment, or the exercise of sanctions, should only arise when there is a failure to use the learning gained from evaluation to seek greater effectiveness. The new approach relies on methods and tools that are accessible—simple, cost effective, and user friendly. Evaluation, in this new way, is a strategic investment.

Examples, by no means exhaustive, of evaluation methods matching the proposed strategy include very simple, inexpensive actions that can be taken by people centrally involved in the program and organization. When everyone engages in evaluative thinking and questioning about what is happening, important learning can occur. Open assessment of observed activities, behaviors, and results, as compared with program objectives, can produce insights that suggest midcourse corrections in the design or execution of a project.

Other current approaches, less scientific but very useful, include *responsive evaluation,* which seeks to answer the questions of the stakeholders by generating information needed for daily decisions in the ongoing execution of the project. "The responsive evaluation . . . trades off some measurement precision in order to increase the usefulness of the findings to persons in and around the program" (Taylor and Sumariwalla, 1992, p. 97). *Naturalistic evaluation* is also appropriate to this concept of evaluation. It has been around for a number of years and has gained renewed interest because it "attempts to arrive at naturalistic generalizations . . . aimed at nontechnical audiences like teachers or the public at large; [it] uses ordinary language; [it] is based on informal everyday reasoning; and [it] makes extensive use of arguments which attempt to establish the structure of reality" (Taylor and Sumariwalla, 1992, p. 98). In addition, much more use could be made of *marketing surveys* to obtain feedback on the effects of an intervention. This includes client, customer, or stakeholder satisfaction surveys, which can generate information that is very helpful in improving the effectiveness of program and organizational initiatives.

For this kind of evaluation to flourish, all stakeholders must operate in a climate of trust. *Partnership* is an appropriate metaphor to characterize relationships among stakeholders. Disclosure of failures as well as successes should be appreciated and should occur in the spirit of learning together. Unless incentives cultivate trust and openness, and cast learning as the objective of evaluation, the new approach cannot take root.

The new approach to evaluation—with its demotion of the report card and with its preference for a model of learning—paints a beautiful picture of organizational growth and harmony. Achieving it is no easy task, however, as it requires a transformation in thought processes based on an organizational setting that rarely exists today. It glosses over the tough problems that could thwart implementation.

NEW MODES OF ORGANIZING

The new approach to ongoing evaluation sketched out here assumes that several characteristics of an organization will be in place. Those ideal attributes crystallize logically from the new approach and from some pioneering experiences with it. In reality, implementation encounters some tough tasks in infusing this new kind of evaluation into an organization's culture and its day-to-day operations. Nonetheless, the pressures on the nonprofit sector intensify the need to demonstrate its impact on our communities and our citizens.

At root, the new evaluation is a normative expression: it puts the spotlight on effectiveness. Implicit in that expression are two other values—excellence in leading and managing the affairs of an organization and ethics in the discharge of mission through programs, projects, and daily operations. To attain these values, ongoing evaluation is the instrument.

An organization where learning is at the core of its routines assumes that trust permeates the relationships among the rank and file, including volunteers and clients. A conventional organization with a fixed hierarchy rarely develops such an atmosphere of trust. Command-and-control structures make trust dangerous, as they turn equals and subordinates into competitors and superiors into taskmasters. If trust is to unleash learning as an ongoing dynamic, there are organizational prerequisites that need to be in place. These prerequisites address the leadership, structure, planning, and inclusiveness of the organization.

Organizational Imperatives

With hierarchy as a point of analytic comparison, the learning model of evaluation envisions leadership that is neither positional nor tactical. Leaders of organizations that practice ongoing evaluation cannot be seen as simply at the apex of the organization chart by virtue of being the CEO or executive director or president. Nor is it sufficient to charge them only with fund raising goals for campaigns. Nor can they afford to be merely charismatic leaders who champion inspirational causes in a community and rally voluntary support. Instead, leaders need to be collaborators and catalysts. If the ordinary, albeit provocative, question of the day is "how are we doing?" a leader needs to be able to hear bad news as well as good news and use that knowledge to inspire the board, the staff, and the volunteers to scrutinize how they might do better. That dynamic dialogue implies that a leader needs to be a learner in a collaborative process of feedback—not just on the strategic and tactical aspects of the organization but also on its ongoing daily activities. The leader needs to be adroit at conversation. *How can we do better?* This question should become the essence of an ongoing dialogue. And when answers disclose shortcomings, even failures, the reaction should not necessarily be reprisal, unless unethical or illegal practices emerge. The stereotypical leadership behavior in a hierarchical organization—predicated on command and control with its system of rewards and sanctions—is inconsistent with the learning model of evaluation. For the new approach to graft onto a nonprofit organization, the leader needs to nurture a climate of trust, of change and caring. The personal and experiential attributes of that leader do not necessarily equate to the seniority system so often attached to the hierarchical traditions of many organizations.

Another organizational prerequisite addresses the structure of the organization, both formally and informally in the pattern of relationships. To be sure, nonprofit organizations tend to deviate from the rigidities of hierarchy because of their reliance on volunteers and because of their often elusive missions. Nonetheless, many do assume these attributes. Their durability tends to promote formality, and the dictates of funders tend to impose structured forms of organizing. The structure presupposed by the new evaluation rests on a team approach, where sharing in learning is essential to discover what works and what does not. The team needs trust within its own ranks, as staff and volunteers trade information and insight with impunity, and it also needs fluidity and flexibility to mix and match the talents of staff and volunteers to the question at hand. Rather than the rigidity and stability that typically accompany hierarchy, the organization needs a capacity to adapt. Learning from ongoing evaluation means that there may well be midcourse corrections in implementing programs and projects to achieve the outcomes sought. From years of experience in helping kids to read, in healing the sick, in eradicating abuse and violence, in inspiring creativity, and in nurturing the spirit, in all these lofty yet critical missions that guide many nonprofit organizations, our knowledge of how to achieve an outcome—our technology, if you will—is at best tentative. By contrast, the hierarchical model implies a well-established technology, predicated on the manufacturing model, whereby an established practice of converting inputs into outputs yields results with a high degree of certainty. In that setting the conventions of a scientific approach rooted in Taylorism—early efficiency studies—make sense. For most of what the nonprofit sector does, however, our approaches in the pursuit of outcomes are far more probabilistic than deterministic. Hence the structure of our organizations needs to adapt and adapt again as improved ways of implementing missions become clearer.

As a corollary, organizations in the independent sector need the capacity to change. Stability has many virtues in the predictability of services for clients or the certainty of performances for patrons and subscribers. Yet the context in which many nonprofit organizations operate today is swiftly changing. The devolution revolution is rearranging responsibilities within the intergovernmental system; the restructuring as well as globalizing of the economy is attenuating the divide between the haves and have-nots; the advent of information breakthroughs is accelerating the exchange of information and ideas—among other jolting influences, these macro phenomena press in on the entire sector and ripple down to the grass roots. More routinely, organizations see ebbs and flows both in their funding and in their constituencies. Adjustments on a recurrent basis—and at times the repositioning of missions—elevate planning as an essential element of the organization. In theory, the new evaluation should foster a forward-looking process and empower the capacity to change. To work in practice, that vision entails planning as an organizational imperative. Continual scanning of the context and of the constituency of the organization is essential. Planning should help ensure that the mission is genuinely ingrained into daily operations.

Another organizational imperative implied by the new evaluation is the principle of inclusiveness. Unlike government (with elections to signal approval or disapproval of performance) and unlike business (with profits and losses to define success and failure), the nonprofit sector has no clear mechanism to calibrate how it does. Evaluation is a surrogate. The process needs to involve all the stakeholders in the enterprise of the mission. For a nonprofit, those stakeholders are numerous and dispersed. They include the board, the professional staff, the volunteers, the philanthropic donors (as well as government), the clients, consumers, patients, patrons, and subscribers, and the community at large. Assessing how well an organization is doing in the discharge of its mission demands an inclusive survey of all the stakeholders.

Tough Tasks

The contemporary literature on management—whether it be total quality management or continuous improvement in business or reinventing or reengineering government—echoes many of these imperatives. As both corporations and governments have discovered on these pathways to reform, organizational change entails some tough tasks. No doubt nonprofit organizations will encounter many of the same tasks as they proceed with implementing the new evaluation. The overarching tough task is perhaps philosophically rooted in some hard questions:

- Does the organization have the moral commitment and ethical courage to ask tough questions?

- Is the organization willing to ask Why are we doing what we are doing?

- Do our activities square with our mission?

- Are we achieving what we aspire to do?

These are the good questions that could potentially yield answers that put an organization out of business or precipitate radical change. They are threatening questions because many people have a vested interest in organizational survival. They are quite unlike past probes for accountability, which employed such questions as how many clients did the homeless shelter serve or how many symphony tickets did the orchestra sell and the like. The questions invoked by the new evaluation have the potential to expose an organization in its very basic existence.

A second tough task in implementing the new evaluation is more pragmatic and organizational in its locus. Historically, past practices of evaluation usually focused on a program or project such as a literacy improvement initiative or a day care center. With the new approach stretching the reach of evaluation to outcomes, it becomes apparent that there are variables beyond the program or project that affect the outcome. A literacy program for children staffed by trained volunteers may operate after school to help shore up proficiency in reading. No matter how many hours of instruction or amounts of resources committed, a complex of variables will shape the results. For example, is there reinforcement for reading at home with regular practice? Does homework from in-school classes emphasize reading? How adequate is the in-school instruction in reading? Is there pressure from peers to read or to rebel? Does the technology of teaching reading make it fun or boring? Is the child healthy enough to devote energy to reading? Evaluation of an initiative such as a learning process for improved literacy should encompass the variables embedded in those questions—yet many are outside the instructional process and the organization itself. These variables extend to networks beyond the formal program of instruction—to the family, to the peers, and to the community. In theory, evaluation should comprehend all these networks and stakeholders. In reality, most nonprofit organizations do not conceptualize this larger framework. To do so is time consuming and resource intensive, let alone intellectually complex. It is far simpler to focus on output measures such as the number of children enrolled and their standardized scores on reading exams.

A third tough task is similarly both organizational and analytic. Given the number and variety of organizations that populate the nonprofit sector, there is no "one best way" to do evaluation. As our colleague Ricardo Millet (1995) of the W. K. Kellogg Foundation has observed, there is "no silver bullet, there is no scientific wizardry." Put another way: there is no established protocol. Millet puts the case simply yet eloquently: "good evaluation is good thinking." In practice, evaluation is asking good questions: What works and why? What doesn't work and why? What have we learned from doing? While there is no one canonized protocol, the very asking of these questions animates tensions within an organization. Because of reliance on philanthropic donations or government support, nonprofit organizations are often held to standards or yardsticks for performance set by the funders. There is then the natural tendency to provide funders with what they want as feedback in the most positive way. There is the understandable inclination to conceal negative information that may signify failure and jeopardize continued funding.

Still another tough task has to do with the rigor of the research in evaluating outcomes, as alluded to earlier in this chapter. The old disciplines of cost-benefit analysis or performance measurement may not be adequate, especially for human and creative services, where perceptions and values are crucially important. The issue of control groups to isolate the effects of an intervention still persists—without identifying two groups and applying the intervention only to one of them, it is hard to state what effects the intervention had, yet it is ethically problematic to identify a group as needing and deserving an intervention and then not give them access to it. And there remains the prickly issue of the definition of outcome measures themselves: do they capture the phenomenon that is the essence of the program or project? Do crime rates adequately diagnose safety? Reading scores, literacy? These are not idle academic questions—they have the potential to affect resources as well as community attitudes. The only honest admonition is that measures are still evolving; the task is one of trial and error. Happily new conventions are adding to our analytic repertoire—benchmarking, best practices, total quality management, and the like.

Finally, among the toughest tasks is to overcome the very threat to an organization posed by evaluation, whether old style or new. Evaluation is a threat to a nonprofit organization because it is costly, it takes time, and it displaces daily operations. As Harry Hatry of the Urban Institute has noted (1995), there is a "dark side" to evaluation. Because funding can be at risk, evaluation can evoke fear in an organization and its stakeholders; it can freeze an organization into risk-averse behavior, and it can lead staff and volunteers to close ranks around the hackneyed refrain "but we do good works." Such reactions expose the endemic distrust between fund seekers and fund grantors and the realpolitik of those relationships.

SUMMARY

The contemporary climate of the nonprofit sector provides a strong incentive to cope with the tough tasks and embrace a more palatable view of evaluation. The stark reality is that funders demand more accountability than an audit of expenditures on allowable items in relation to activities undertaken can provide. Perhaps spearheaded by the scandals at United Way of America or New Era Philanthropy or occasioned by cutbacks and contractions in government—or precipitated by the reshuffling of intergovernmental roles—whatever complex calculus is at work, the nonprofit sector can no longer invoke "good works" as its mantra. While most nonprofits still try to do so, a number have begun to look for ways to cite real results. Increasingly, demonstrating worth will be the price of philanthropy.

References

Gray, S. T. (ed.). *A Vision of Evaluation.* Washington, D.C.: INDEPENDENT SECTOR, 1993.

Hatry, H. Remarks at the initial meeting of the Task Force on Impact of United Way of America, Alexandria, Va., Summer 1995.

Millet, R. Remarks at the annual meeting of the American Evaluation Society, Vancouver, B.C., October 1995.

Taylor, M. E., and Sumariwalla, R. D. In D. R. Young, V. A. Hodgkinson, R. M. Hollister, and Associates, *Governing, Leading, and Managing Nonprofit Organizations: New Insights from Research and Practice.* San Francisco: Jossey-Bass, 1992.

Waldrop, M. M. *Complexity.* New York: Simon & Schuster, 1992.

CHAPTER SEVEN

Program Effectiveness and Outcomes

John A. Seeley

program—that is, an integrated set of activities and resources with explicit goals—makes a useful unit for evaluation. It is much more nearly self-contained than an organization or an activity, and is thus easier to study. This chapter offers a set of questions that can guide an ongoing learning process focused on producing information useful to program stakeholders. The questions are intended to be adaptable to the many types of programs in the many types of organizations that make up the independent sector. Although they provide a good start on the process, these questions do not in themselves constitute a "how to" guide. Readers interested in practical applications will find other useful tips elsewhere in this volume and in the literature of evaluation.

The chapter is organized into four sections. The first, on context, suggests why the topic of program effectiveness and outcomes is critical to the performance of the independent sector. The second identifies six key elements of program effectiveness and offers questions related to each, while the third, on program results, discusses the differences between outputs, outcomes, and impacts, and offers some questions to shape clear thinking about results. The final section provides a summary and overview, and another short list of questions.

BACKGROUND AND CONTEXT

The independent sector comprises many types of institutions, including foundations, cultural institutions, associations, and service delivery organizations, all of which serve the public interest one way or another. Programming in the sector knows few boundaries. *Funding, education, research, voluntary action, advocacy,* and *direct service* suggest the variety of programmatic initiatives.

Nonprofit institutions are being called upon by many different political interests to play an enhanced and increasingly visible role in the quality of community life and the solution of community problems. The independent sector has become an increasingly strong magnet for hope, attention, research, and both fiscal and ethical accountability. While expectations are increasing, resources are not. "Do more with less" is heard as often as "work smarter, not harder." Hopes for an improved quality of life for all people—plus specific performance expectations for institutions in the sector—are being translated into new and reaffirmed missions and programs. The sector shows renewed energy and momentum.

In addition to these expectations, another set of influences is shaping the sector. Changing demographics, both nationally and regionally, affect both who is served and who is employed by nonprofits. The proportion of people from non-white ethnic backgrounds is increasing. We are living longer and we are moving about in our states and regions. The distribution of public funds is changing, with block grants and welfare reform receiving political attention. Technology continues to influence the way we communicate, and the way we acquire, digest, and report information. Simply put, the sector is in flux.

Trends and issues in the field of assessment or evaluation also affect the sector. At least three trends are clear. The quest for responsible self-evaluation represented by the INDEPENDENT SECTOR's work on *A Vision of Evaluation* (Gray, 1993) is one. The influence of "continuous improvement," generated most visibly by the business community but known to evaluators as formative evaluation, is another. And finally, the emphasis on assessing program outcomes, as articulated currently by the United Way and other funders, is a powerful spur to activity in the area.

The professional evaluation community, while built on a strong conceptual, methodological, and ethical foundation, struggles with old and new issues as well. Is causation or contribution a more appropriate way to think about the impact of programs? What values lie behind the difference? What is the proper combination of qualitative and quantitative methods and evidence to portray effectiveness usefully, accurately, and in a culturally sensitive way? In what ways are the profession's current standards applicable in an increasingly self-evaluating sector?

In short, the independent sector is being shaped by rising expectations for performance, by demographic, funding, and technological trends, and by assessment issues. The factors create wonderful opportunities and bring with them very strong challenges to the performance and credibility of the nonprofit world. One highly responsible way to chart a course into the next century is by asking the right questions of organizations or programs. Identifying good questions is not enough, however. Gathering information, reflecting upon it, and communicating effectively about it are also key ingredients of performance improvement.

PROGRAM EFFECTIVENESS

What contributes to effective programming? This is a good question to keep at the forefront. Answers may vary to some extent across the nonprofit world because institutions operate in different contexts and programs operate in varying organizational cultures. In general, however, creating and adapting an effective program model is the answer. An effective program model integrates six key elements, as follows:

- Discernible community needs to address or assets to strengthen
- Clear and integrated organizational and programmatic mission, goals, and objectives
- Activities logically connected to accomplishing the program goals and objectives
- A management structure appropriate for the goals and activities
- Human and material resources sufficient to implement the program at a level that will achieve the goals in the expected time period
- Measurable performance indicators

A program has to be both well designed and well implemented to be effective. An effective design includes the logical connections among community needs and assets, program goals, and program activities, resources, and management structure. These connections represent the basic logical or intuitive flow of the program. In other words, the model asks and answers one comprehensive question: If we create and do these things, is it likely that what we want to have happen will happen?

In addition to program design issues, there are program implementation issues. These concern how well and how fully the program is carried out in practice. For example, if a promising program isn't working, you may find that the staff is doing the right things but not doing them well. Or the staff may be doing the right things and doing them well, but without enough hands to meet the needs and accomplish the goals. These are both implementation and not design issues. Figures 7.1 and 7.2 offer a simplistic summary of the approach.

This model embodies the following logic: specific needs or assets in the community or in an organization suggest that the following program goals and objectives are a sound response, and therefore the following activities are required to accomplish goals. A management structure of (thus and such) is

Community needs/assets	Program mission goals/ objectives	Program activities	Program management	Program resources	Program performance indicators

Figure 7.1. Program Model.

necessary to operate the program, and the program design will require the following kinds of resources to be successful: (a, b, c . . .). Our success indicators related directly or indirectly to the goals and objectives and implementation of the program include (x, y, z . . .).

Whether portrayed as a linear path or a different but instructive model, Figure 7.1 focuses attention on the connections between what is needed, what is to be done, what is to be accomplished, and what indicators suggest success. Figure 7.2 emphasizes that sound logic is only a partial contributor to effectiveness. Effective implementation is the other key ingredient. The four cells in Figure 7.2 suggest that design quality and implementation effectiveness interact to contribute to overall program performance.

With this as a basic starting point in how to think about programming, what questions might inform responsible assessment of program design and program effectiveness? Exhibit 7.1 offers examples of questions born from this author's experience. Each element of the program model is identified on the left, as are the design and implementation components of effective programming. Sample questions are suggested on the right. Some questions could fit in both the design and performance categories—but it is more important to ask the question and get the answer than to figure out precisely what category it belongs in.

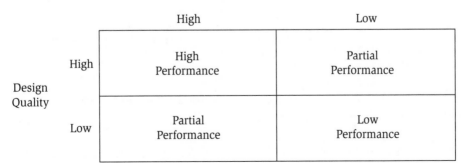

Implementation Effectiveness

		High	Low
Design Quality	High	High Performance	Partial Performance
	Low	Partial Performance	Low Performance

Figure 7.2. Program Performance.

Program Model Dimension	
Needs and Assets	**Sample Questions**
Design Questions	What is the vision and mission of the organization?
	To what extent do community members, organizational leaders, and staff share in the mission?
	How closely do the needs and assets to which we want to respond fit our vision and mission?
	How extensive are the needs and assets? Are they of sufficient significance and number for us to respond to them?
	What factors in the environment influence the nature and extent of these needs and assets?
	Who are the program stakeholders? How should they be involved in the program design process?
Implementation Questions	To what extent is our mission still important in light of our changing environment?
	To what extent is our mission supported by key stakeholders such as community members, organizational leaders, and our own staff?
	To what extent are our programs linked effectively to our mission?
	To what extent are we discharging our mission effectively?

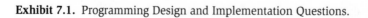

Exhibit 7.1. Programming Design and Implementation Questions.

Goals and Objectives	Sample Questions
Design Questions	Are the goals clearly related to the mission and needs and assets to which they respond?
	To what extent are the goals clear and measurable?
	What are the most significant indicators of goal achievement?
Implementation Questions	To what extent are the goals understood and shared by the stakeholders?
	To what extent are the goals being accomplished?
	To what extent are our customers satisfied with the services and products we offer?

Activities	Sample Questions
Design Questions	What are the activities necessary to accomplish the goals and objectives?
	How can they best be integrated with each other and sequenced to achieve the goals?
	What amount of activity is necessary to accomplish the goals in the time expected?
Implementation Questions	Are the activities being implemented as planned?
	To what extent are the activities integrated and sequenced effectively?
	To what extent is each activity effective?
	How can the activities be improved?

(continued)

Program Model Dimension	
Management	**Sample Questions**
Design Questions	What are the types of management decisions required to operate the program?
	Who should be empowered to make these decisions?
	What about the program needs to be communicated to whom and how frequently?
Implementation Questions	To what extent is the management of the program effective?

Resources	**Sample Questions**
Design Questions	What kinds of resources—human, material, financial, technological—are necessary to operate the program?
	Are they being acquired and used as planned?
Implementation Questions	Are there sufficient resources in use to operate the program?
	What is the quality of the resources?
	To what extent is the staff performing effectively?
	How could our use of our resources, including our efficiency, be improved?

Performance Indicators	Sample Questions
Design Questions	Who should be involved in identifying the indicators?
	Should the evaluation of performance include intended and unintended outcomes?
	How can the indicators be measured?
	What is the measurement plan?
	Who should be involved in reflecting on the collected information?
Implementation Questions	To what extent was the evaluation plan implemented?
	How effective was the plan in terms of the usefulness of results, the feasibility of the design, the propriety with which it was conducted, and the accuracy of the information provided?

This section has focused on how to think about programming and the questions that might help guide its assessment. Six key elements of programming were identified, and the concepts of design success and implementation success were discussed. Both have to be present to maximize programming effectiveness. The next section suggests ways of thinking about program results.

PROGRAM RESULTS

In recent years the notion of measuring program results has gained prominence. Why measure results? Asking and answering this question clearly is critical for each organization and its programs within the independent sector. Without knowing clearly why the question should be answered, precious resources can be wasted. Some common reasons for measuring results include accountability to those served and to the board, funders, and so on; improvement to enhance effectiveness; understanding to inform reflective practice; and documentation to foster thoughtful replication. Any organization may have its own special mix of these and other reasons. Assessing results is a natural part of effective programming and is most successful when integrated into an ongoing process of institutional and programmatic evaluation and learning.

This section provides ways of thinking about program results, thinking that will lead to the creation of questions that facilitate the achievement of program goals. The field of evaluation is unsettled on how best to think about results, but three types of program results—outputs, outcomes, and impacts—are becoming prominent in both theory and practice.

Outputs

Outputs are quantitative indicators of what the program actually does: the number of clients it serves, the number of grants it awards, the number of members it recruits, the number and types of research projects it funds. Outputs are the quantitative evidence of the activity component of the program model. The underlying logic suggests that if certain activities are done well, the desired results will occur. Outputs can be distinguished from *inputs*, which are the resources of money, time, materials, facilities, and energy that we put into programs. In some situations the measurement of outputs serves as a proxy measure for more substantial results. Sample questions:

- What did we actually do as part of this program?
- How did we spend our time?
- How many people did we serve?
- Who were these people?

Outcomes

The term *outcomes* indicates a focus on the observable changes in individuals, institutions, conditions, services, policies, processes, products, and so on linked to the objectives and activities of the program. Usually, *desired outcomes*—the ones suggested in the mission statement and so on—are those measured. However, attention to identifying *unintended outcomes* also promotes accountability, improvement, understanding, and replication. Immediate outcomes are the results of the program that can be most closely linked to it. Frequently, they are caused directly by the program. Here are some typical questions:

- To what extent did we accomplish our goals?
- What are the unintended results of this program?

- For whom was the program most successful?
- To what extent do the outcomes measure up to our expectations or standards?
- How can we achieve more or better outcomes?

Impacts

The term *impacts* is often thought of as referring to the longer-term, community-based results of the program. One program's outcomes can become a contributor to a continuum of care and a larger mosaic of outcomes that contribute to improvements in the quality of life for a community. Quality of life indicators, including economic, educational, health, family, and neighborhood indicators, inform the assessment of impact. Here are some sample questions:

- What do we mean by the quality of life?
- To what extent is the quality of life improving in this community? Why or why not?
- What is the contribution of this program to improving the quality of life?

Outcomes Measurement

Measuring outcomes in nonprofit organizations often meets with considerable resistance. This is understandable and can be expected. Often program practitioners absorbed in daily activity feel that the rush to measure outcomes is someone else's thing. It is being done to them, not with them. Those responsible for outcomes measurement often accept its potential value, but believe that the results they seek are simply beyond measurement. Resistance often occurs because those responsible have not yet acquired the knowledge and skills necessary to engage in useful evaluation. While resistance is natural, however, people all over the country are successfully coming to terms with outcomes measurement. Handbooks and training sessions are appearing. Ongoing evaluation appears in conference programs with increasing regularity. Outcomes measurement is becoming acknowledged as worthwhile and feasible.

Outcomes measurement is both worthwhile and feasible, but there are four related issues that are troublesome—though in no way insurmountable. First, in the rush to measure and focus on outcomes, the purposes of continuous learning and improvement may be lost. Second, an overreliance on quantitative measures may divert attention from understanding why the outcomes occurred and the meaning of the outcomes for individuals, organizations, and the larger community. Third, the pressures of accountability and a quick assessment may not produce information that is of sufficient quality to be trusted, or that is useful to key stakeholders who have not been involved in its development. Fourth, in the rush to get on board, organization or program management may be tempted to start from scratch in building an outputs measurement system. This is unnecessary. Many resources and talents are emerging to facilitate the assessment of program effectiveness and outcomes.

SUMMARY

This chapter has suggested ways to think about assessing program effectiveness and outcomes. It identified six key elements of program design, including the identification of community needs and assets, the creation of program goals, program activities, and management structure, the acquisition of resources, and the creation of outcomes indicators. It also pointed out the need to distinguish between the quality of a program design and the effectiveness of program implementation—and to work for excellence in both areas. Many questions related to overall effectiveness were offered as starting points in an ongoing learning process.

Three types of program results were identified: program outputs, outcomes, and impacts. While outcomes measurement is demanding and will be met with some resistance, it is a critical ingredient in the ongoing assessment process.

Systematic assessment based on thoughtful questions can guide both program improvement and accountability. It will contribute substantially to effective practice if we continuously ask and answer these questions:

- Is this organization and program doing the right things in pursuit of its mission?
- To what extent are our programs effectively implemented?
- What are the results of our efforts?
- How can our programs be improved?

Reference

Gray, S. T. (ed.). *A Vision of Evaluation*. Washington, D.C.: INDEPENDENT SECTOR, 1993.

CHAPTER EIGHT

Human Resource Management

Dennis R. Young
Humphrey Doermann

Nonprofit organizations operate principally in the services sector of the economy. As a result, their performance depends much more on the quality of the work done by their people than on the efficiency of their equipment or the structure of their buildings. Therefore, if nonprofit organizations are to effectively monitor how well they are performing and what they must do to renew themselves over time, they must necessarily focus their attention on continuous evaluation and improvement of their workforces. This applies as much to their volunteers as their paid staff.

The long-run growth and performance of any organization depends on building and maintaining *capital*, that is, those input resources the organization requires so as to be able to produce its output efficiently over time. In business, we typically think of capital as manifested in buildings, major equipment, and financial resources. In nonprofits, however, *human capital* is the overwhelmingly important form of capital, and "the essence of human capital is that investments are made in human resources so as to improve their productivity" (Pearce, 1995). The concept of human capital reminds us not only that it requires investment in the form of education and other means, but also that human capacity can depreciate or become obsolete if not properly maintained or renewed. Evaluating human resources in a nonprofit organization thus requires that attention be given to the *processes* through which the capacity of people, as individuals and as groups, is maintained and improved over time.

LEVELS OF HUMAN RESOURCE MANAGEMENT

The concept of human capital applies not only to the skills and talents of individuals in the workforce but also to the processes and relationships in an organization that allow people to work together in an effective way. For the purpose of this discussion, it is convenient to divide human capital into three categories—individual, team, and organization:

- *Individual* capital refers to the talents, energy, creativity, knowledge, and skills of individual volunteers and paid staff members that contribute positively to the work of the organization.
- *Team* capital refers to the relationships, habits, practices, and procedures that have developed among members of working groups in the organization (departments, projects, task forces, and so on) that enable the people in those groups to work effectively together.
- *Organization* capital refers to the supportive resources, systems, and processes that the organization uses to ensure that individual capital and team capital are renewed and enhanced over time.

Clearly, the three types of human capital are interdependent. Individual capital can only be preserved and improved within a supportive organization. Team capital depends on capable individuals who work well in a group. And so on. However, at each of these levels, the maintenance and development of human capital requires focusing on somewhat different issues and concerns. These issues suggest a core of questions that nonprofits must ask themselves as they evaluate their human resource capacities and performance at each level.

There are also certain common factors that affect all three categories of human capital in nonprofit organizations. One such factor is the pervasiveness of change. To stand still in a rapidly moving world is to deteriorate. Thus, continuous evaluation and reinvestment in human capital is required not only to compensate for wear and tear and the need for rest, repair, and recuperation (just as machines need maintenance and occasional new parts), but also to avoid obsolescence. Nonprofits operate in a variety of fast-moving professional fields and social environments in which current knowledge and skills are critical to continued effectiveness. Individuals, teams, and the organizations as a whole must respond to constantly shifting environments or be lost in the wake of change.

A key aspect of change affecting human capital is the increasing importance of cultural diversity. In the United States and elsewhere, the workforce as well as the constituencies of nonprofit organizations are fast becoming highly heterogeneous. The growing participation of women in the workforce, the aging of the population, and the increasing participation of many different ethnic and racial groups in society as a whole, present challenges of a magnitude to human capital development never before faced. These challenges manifest themselves in several important ways, including the imperative for nonprofits to find ways to exploit the multiple contributions that people of diverse backgrounds can make to the productivity of an organization and to overcome the frictions that prevent diverse people from working effectively together.

HUMAN RESOURCES AND EVALUATION

This section takes the perspective of a chief executive officer or a director of human resources responsible for ensuring maximum effectiveness of a nonprofit organization's paid and volunteer workforces. To evaluate the efficacy of current organizational policies and procedures, such an official needs to focus on a number of salient dimensions of human resource practice, pose the right questions about the execution and effects of those practices, and marshal information that will facilitate decisions leading to continuous improvement of workforce performance. The appropriate questions and information requirements differ among the three categories of human capital, but the general process of evaluation and assessment is the same—ask the right questions and seek improvements based on information collected to answer those questions.

At the individual level, the challenges to nonprofits are to identify people with appropriate talents and interests, place them effectively within the organization, and shape their assignments to best employ their abilities. It is also necessary to provide the educational opportunities that will allow people to become more productive over time, reward or discipline people appropriately and treat them fairly, and provide for their individual advancement within appropriate career scenarios.

At the team level, the challenges involve assembling the right combinations of people to work together, maintaining successful teams and making adjustments to less successful ones, and devising and monitoring practices to ensure successful coordination among team members and high morale for the team as a whole. The challenges also include developing appropriate leadership within teams and balancing the needs of individual team members with those of the team as a whole.

At the organization level, the challenges are to develop and maintain the appropriate systems and policies to ensure that the quality of individual personnel and the effectiveness of organizational teams are maintained and improved over the long run. These considerations include appropriate recruitment strategies, evaluation procedures, promotion and reward systems, educational and training opportunities, and conflict resolution capabilities.

For purposes of ongoing evaluation and continuous improvement, the kinds of questions the chief executive or human resource director must ask flow directly from the foregoing concerns at the three levels, and the interactions among those levels. In the next sections, we identify many of the important questions. Since the questions apply to both paid and volunteer workforces, we use the term *staff member* generically to encompass both. Following this exposition, we will also indicate where it is important to make distinctions between paid staff and volunteers in assessing the answers to these questions.

Evaluation of Individuals

Organizations typically provide employees with performance reviews, usually on an annual basis, often connected with decisions about compensation or advancement, and commonly restricted to paid workers. While a well-designed performance evaluation helps a supervisor coach individuals on improving their work as well as make compensation and promotion decisions about them, the scope of such an evaluation may be far too restrictive to encompass all the important facets of individual performance and development. The questions one should ask about individual workers begin before they enter employment and end only after they leave the organization. In between, the questions should focus on how the worker is developing, how productive he or she has become, and how well he or she fits into the organization's schema, now and in the future. All these considerations apply to volunteer as well as paid staff.

To take a roughly chronological approach, the following queries apply at the recruitment stage:

- *What are the special skills, knowledge, and talents of the prospective staff member?* How do they compare with other prospective candidates? Will they enhance the productivity of the organization? Will the candidate be able to use and develop these skills within this organization?
- *What factors motivate the prospective staff member?* Are the organization's mission and resources consistent with that motivation? What career scenario does the individual envision? Is that scenario consistent with working and advancing in this organization?
- *How well does the prospective staff member work with other people?* Can the nature of work in this organization accommodate the candidate's preferences for individual versus team effort?

The following queries apply at the periodic (annual) assessment stage:

- *Has the staff member been placed into a team or department that best accommodates his or her talents and interests?* What value has the individual added to the work of that department or to the organization as a whole? Are there cultural factors that inhibit communications between the staff member and other workers? If so, what can be done to ameliorate such constraints?

- *Are the individual's developmental goals being met?* What work experiences within the organization, or internal or external education or training opportunities, can be provided to promote that development more effectively?
- *How has the staff member been rewarded for his or her performance, financially or otherwise?* Has that reward been commensurate with his or her contributions to the organization? Is there a more cost-effective way (some other combination of rewards or benefits) to recognize the individual's contributions within the context of the organization's resource constraints?
- *Does the staff member feel that he or she has been treated fairly?* Are there outstanding grievances that have not been satisfactorily resolved? If so, are there additional pathways that can be explored to resolve those issues? Does the individual harbor feelings of discrimination? If so, what can be done to sensitize other staff members to this situation?
- *Does the staff member's job description accurately reflect what he or she is actually doing?* Should it be amended to recognize additional capabilities, new limitations, or changes in organizational requirements?
- *Is the staff member ready for additional responsibilities?* Are there opportunities for promotion within the organization for which the individual should receive consideration? Has a practical scenario for advancement been identified that can serve as a guide for the individual's development?

The following queries apply at the retirement or termination stage:

- *What are the reasons for leaving?* Does this represent a positive opportunity for the individual, a natural change, or the termination of a troubled employment relationship?
- *What suggestions does the individual have for improvements in the way the organization manages its workforce?* What help can the individual provide for recruiting future staff to the organization?
- *How can the organization honor the individual for his or her career with the organization?* Is there a way to maintain future communications?

Evaluation of Teams

The work of an organization is often carried out by groups of individuals who must interact closely with one another to produce a common output. These teams may be formally organized along departmental lines or through cross-functional task forces, or less formally around particular projects or tasks. As every sports team manager or music conductor knows, putting a good team together and having it function well for a long time is a tremendous challenge. It involves questions of selection and compatibility of team members, skillful coordination, attention to group morale, and appropriate and effective leadership. These considerations are the basis of questions for the continuing evaluation of organizational teams:

- *Do staff belonging to the team possess the right combination of skills and talents to maximize team performance?* If not, what are the weak spots, what additional skills are needed, and what changes in team composition should be made?

- *Are the procedures (meetings, practice sessions, operating manuals, standard rules of operation, and so on) for coordinating the efforts of team members as effective as they can be?* What changes are needed in current procedures, what additional procedures may be required, and what procedures are unnecessarily constraining and can be eliminated?

- *What is tenor of group morale?* Are spirits high? Is the group unified in its feelings or is there internal dissension? What are the sources of dissension or low morale? Are there mechanisms in place for the group to address these concerns in a constructive way?

- *How are individuals rewarded for the success of the group or penalized for its failures?* Are there opportunities for individuals within the group to shine and receive special recognition for their contributions? How are individual incentives for recognition balanced against potentials for resentment if some individuals receive more attention than others?

- *How is leadership manifested within the group?* Are individuals appropriately recognized or rewarded for their leadership? What role does leadership play in successfully coordinating group efforts and achieving high morale? Is the current leadership a factor in group success or are changes in leadership suggested?

Evaluation of Organizational Capacity

While the work of an organization gets done by individuals and teams, it falls to the top leadership and administration of the organization to ensure that the policies and systems are in place to properly support those individuals and teams over time. It is at this level that an emphasis must be put on building the infrastructure of continuing evaluation and assessment of the organization's human capital. In addition, the organization must have strategic policies and capacities to ensure the long-run maintenance and investment in that capital. Hence, the following questions are pertinent to the continuing evaluation of the organization's human resource functions as a whole:

- *What mechanisms and resources are in place to identify and recruit new talent to the organization?* How do these capacities ensure that the organization reaches out effectively to all relevant population groups? What information is being collected to document and assess both the cultural diversity and the talents of the organization's workforce over time?

- *What educational and training programs and policies are in place to help ensure that the organization's workers can upgrade their skills?* What information is being collected to measure the use of such developmental opportunities and their impact on organizational productivity and individual advancement?

• *What policies, procedures, and resources exist to ensure that workers receive fair and impartial hearings of their grievances or amelioration of their conflicts?* What information is collected to assess how frequently these resources are used, how well they are regarded, and how effectively they work?

• *What policies, programs, and resources are in place to ensure that individuals and groups are recognized and rewarded in a manner that is commensurate with their performance and fairly administered throughout the organization?* What information is being collected to determine whether the organization's compensation policies are competitive with those of other organizations in its field? What information is assembled to determine if workers within the organization perceive compensation and reward policies as fair and productive?

• *What policies and programs exist to delineate alternate career paths and modes of advancement within the organization?* What information is collected to examine the use and desirability of these career paths? What policies and principles guide the selection of inside versus outside candidates for vacancies in the organization? What information is collected to assess the success or failure of these policies over time?

VOLUNTEERS VERSUS PAID STAFF

The foregoing evaluation questions apply generically to both paid and volunteer workforces, and to mixes of the two. Nonetheless, it is also important to recognize that volunteers and paid workers have different strengths and weaknesses, and that human resource development strategies must recognize these differences. It is not so much that different questions must be asked about these groups as that we must expect different answers and we must analyze the resultant information according to somewhat different criteria. A perusal of the foregoing lists of questions suggests the following differences:

• Certain staff positions may be more effectively filled by paid staff members and others more effectively filled by volunteers.

• The motivations for work may differ, on average, between paid and volunteer workers.

• The developmental goals of volunteers are likely to be different from those of paid staff.

• The issues of discrimination are likely to be different for volunteers than for paid staff. In particular, volunteers may feel they are treated as less important within the organization because they are not being paid.

Or staff may feel abused by volunteers whom they may view as unaccountable.

- Teams may be more effective with some combinations of volunteers and paid staff than with other combinations.
- Certain types of reward or compensation may be more appropriate for paid staff than for volunteers and vice versa.
- Certain types of fringe benefits and developmental opportunities may be more appropriate for paid staff than for volunteers and vice versa.
- The employment contracts and job descriptions of volunteers versus paid workers will necessarily differ in certain respects.
- The career scenarios for volunteers are necessarily different from those of paid staff.
- The reasons and circumstances of leaving the workforce may differ substantially between paid and volunteer workers.
- The policies and procedures guiding hiring, firing, evaluation, and advancement may necessarily differ in certain ways for volunteer versus paid workers.
- The avenues and processes for recruiting volunteers are different from those applying to paid staff.

The existence of these differences does not imply wholly different approaches to human resource evaluation for paid staff and volunteers. On the contrary, nonprofit organizations can be most effective by viewing paid and volunteer workers through essentially the same lens of human capital development and placing these two groups of workers on an equal footing for purposes of management and evaluation. The value of recognizing the differences between volunteers and paid workers is twofold, however. First, it makes explicit the potential for comparing policies for one group against the other. Why is one process or practice being followed for paid workers and not for volunteers? Should a change be made or are there good reasons for treating volunteers differently from paid workers in certain aspects of human resource practice? For example, what kinds of rewards are more appropriate for volunteers than paid staff, and vice versa? Should volunteers qualify for the same kinds of developmental and other benefits as paid workers? Should volunteers have the same kind of employment contracts and job descriptions as paid workers, and be subject to the same policies for hiring, firing, evaluation, and advancement? The answers to these questions may differ from one organization to another, but all organizations can profit by asking them.

Second, the dual focus on paid workers and volunteers allows one to ask how these groups can best be combined to achieve organizational objectives more effectively than either group could do alone. In particular, which positions are more appropriately filled by volunteers and which by paid staff? When should volunteers be considered for paid work opportunities and when can paid staff be asked to volunteer? And what combinations of paid workers and volunteers work best in teams?

In essence, the distinction between volunteers and paid staff leads to the formulation of an additional set of evaluative questions for leaders of nonprofit organizations to address in conjunction with the maintenance and development of their human resources. As the nation's paid workforce ages and becomes more female and less white, the supply of both paid and volunteer workers—and the requirements of those workers—will necessarily change over time. Thus, especially at the organization-wide level, the policies applying differentially, in combination, and commonly to these two groups must be continually reviewed in light of these trends.

SUMMARY AND PERSPECTIVE

People are the most important form of capital for nonprofit organizations. The maintenance and development of human capital requires that organizational leaders continually assess the decisions, practices, procedures, and systems that are used to manage this resource. Human capital exists at three levels—the individual, the team, and the organization as a whole. At each of these levels, a set of critical questions must periodically be asked to ascertain how well the organization is functioning in its responsibilities to maintain and enhance its volunteer and paid workforces. The answers to these questions should form the basis for continually reexamining and revising organizational practices. In most instances, such information can be shared in a manner that itself enhances the human resource development process.

Assessment information at the individual level can and should be shared between worker and supervisor before such information is acted upon. Information at the team level should be shared and discussed among team members to empower them to improve team functioning. Evaluative information on the organization-wide processes and resources for human resource management should be widely discussed and considered before systemic changes are made. The sharing of information and participation in decisions to adjust policies and practices itself is a form of human capital investment from which the nonprofit organization is likely to reap important dividends.

References

Beer, M., and Spector, B. (eds.). *Reading in Human Resources Management.* New York: Free Press, 1985.

Brudney, J. L. *Fostering Volunteer Programs in the Public Sector: Planning, Initiating, and Managing Voluntary Activities.* San Francisco: Jossey-Bass, 1990.

Pearce, D. W. (ed.). *The MIT Dictionary of Modern Economics.* (4th ed.) Cambridge, Mass.: MIT Press, 1995.

Young, D. R., Hodgkinson, V. A., Hollister, R. M., and Associates. *Governing, Leading, and Managing Nonprofit Organizations: New Insights from Research and Practice.* San Francisco: Jossey-Bass, 1992.

CHAPTER NINE

Information Management

Ricardo A. Millett
Mark A. Lelle

The nonprofit organizations that survive in the twenty-first century will be those that can identify the information needs of their key stakeholders, formulate evaluation questions that allow them to collect information that is both timely and relevant, and use this information to make better management decisions. Organizations that hope to *prosper* will need to develop mechanisms for storing, retrieving, sharing, and analyzing information so that staff, board members, and volunteers can shape the future of their organizations by understanding the present and building on lessons of the past. In other words, they will need to develop management information systems that give them a strong sense of where they have been, where they are, where they want to go, and what they will need to do to get there.

Contrary to general perception, management information systems are not useful and available only to large, financially stable organizations. If anything, effective information management is even more critical for the multitude of small, community-based organizations that populate the third sector—and it is equally available to them. With these organizations in mind, we begin this chapter with a definition of information management that is appropriate for nonprofit organizations of all sizes. We then address the benefits of information management by drawing upon lessons learned from years of work with W. K. Kellogg Foundation grantees, as well as our own experiences as nonprofit executives, board members, volunteers, and evaluators. We conclude this chapter by outlining important elements of management information systems, and by discussing ways that organizations can overcome the barriers to implementing such systems.

WHAT IS INFORMATION MANAGEMENT?

The INDEPENDENT SECTOR publication *A Vision of Evaluation* (Gray, 1993) emphasizes that evaluation and information management are inextricably linked. If evaluation is a thinking skill that involves asking good questions (Sanders, 1993), then information management requires making sure that answers to those questions are available to the people who need them, when they need them, in a usable form.

Simply stated, management information systems (MIS) are the *procedures* used to collect, record, store, retrieve, tabulate, and report data (Cohen and Ooms, 1993). It is important to note that this definition says nothing about computers, spreadsheets, or relational databases, even though they are often used in MIS. For many small nonprofit organizations, a properly maintained file cabinet may be the central component of a management information system—as long as the organizational culture rewards the full use of the information it contains. Conversely, many organizations with powerful computers and vast technological expertise fail to implement effective management information systems because the practical use of information is not part of their mind-set.

Overemphasis on the *means* of information management rather than on the *uses* of information leads to the development of systems that overwhelm common sense and manageability (Buhl, 1996). Information management is a process, a way of thinking that emphasizes the value and power of good information, and this way of thinking must permeate the entire organization.

WHY IS INFORMATION MANAGEMENT IMPORTANT?

Timely, accurate information has a number of benefits depending on the current and anticipated needs of the organization. This section outlines and illustrates the major benefits. It describes each benefit in the context of a different organization, but that is merely a device to make them easier to see. Successful nonprofit organizations can recognize and capitalize on these benefits simultaneously.

- *High-quality information allows organizations to improve the efficiency and effectiveness with which they conduct their operations and deliver services.* If nothing else, the use of good information leads to a state of continuous improvement. Sanders (1993) goes so far as to say that organizational improvement cannot occur without it.

Example: Operation G.R.A.D., a Battle Creek, Michigan–based high school completion program for dropouts, implemented a comprehensive evaluation process that revealed a number of barriers to program success. These included inadequate facilities, a centralized decision-making process, and a highly structured curriculum. Based on the information collected during the evaluation, Operation G.R.A.D. identified instructional facilities that met the educational and social needs of students, allowed teachers greater authority in running meetings and shaping the program, and found a proper balance between classroom teaching and self-paced computer instruction. These improvements led to increases in the number of participants, greater retention of participants, improvements in academic performance, greater retention of teachers, and a decrease in the per-pupil costs of operating the program. The collection, analysis, and dissemination of information that resulted in these positive impacts was possible because the organizational culture placed a high value on using information to guide programmatic change.

- *Information helps organizations develop an institutional memory of what worked (and what didn't) and under what conditions.* This organizational history documents the reasoning that undergirds decisions, and provides a starting point for the design of future programs and initiatives. This is especially valuable in organizations that experience a high rate of turnover among staff and volunteers. Buhl (1996) claims that if evaluation and information management does not promote personal and institutional learning, organizations are "paying for a largely empty exercise."

Example: The W. K. Kellogg Foundation conducted a "lessons learned" conference to collect and synthesize important findings from prior programming. The intent of this process was to help the foundation mine the wealth of its experience and avoid reinventing the wheel when it designed new initiatives. The process was decidedly low tech. Written information related to a variety of themes of interest to the foundation was submitted by cluster evaluators prior to the conference. A synthesis of this information conducted by foundation staff resulted in a concept paper that was further refined by the cluster evaluators and foundation staff who attended the conference.

In contrast to this low-tech process, the W. K. Kellogg Foundation is now developing a computerized system that will collect and analyze data from many of the foundation's community-based health projects. This interactive system will allow grantees from around the country to enter, manage, and transmit information of interest to projects and to the foundation.

This system aims to enhance the capacity of community-based organizations to manage their programs by monitoring changes in data related to their operation. At the same time, it is intended to facilitate the compilation of reports that effectively tell the story of organizational activities and document their unique challenges and successes in creating healthier communities, and to systematically compile community health information that could help guide future grant making at the W. K. Kellogg Foundation.

- *Good information proves to funders and other stakeholders that organizations are worth what it costs to operate them.* Today's donors are disinclined to give because of the simple charity appeal of a cause. Rather, they want to invest their money in nonprofit organizations that are making—and can *demonstrate* that they are making—a real difference in people's lives.

Example: Greater Albion Habitat for Humanity, an Albion, Michigan, affiliate of a national housing organization for low-income families, used outcome information to demonstrate the impact of its work. Because the organization had no computers, volunteers used note cards to compile information about their work—the impact of construction activity on the local economy, increases in city property tax revenues as a result of home construction, increases in the purchasing power of Habitat families due to their reduced housing costs, and improvements in family functioning as a result of a more stable home environment. By collecting and disseminating good outcome information, the affiliate significantly increased private donations to the organization, recruited additional volunteers to the cause, and encouraged local units of government to provide the organization with land on which to build additional houses.

Another benefit of information management that has received considerable attention in the past two years is that MIS allow organizations to capture and mine the wealth of their experiences for the benefit of the field of practice. Good information produced at the community level helps fill the gap between practical experience and the theories developed by academic institutions and policy think tanks. Further, it helps us understand what can be reasonably expected from social programs, and helps us identify better indicators to determine whether we are truly making a difference in terms of our programs' intended outcomes.

Increasingly, organizations are participating in family-centered systems reform initiatives that involve several organizations working together to meet the complex needs of children and families. These comprehensive community initiatives often call for the collection, synthesis, and reporting of information that is uniform across all participating organizations. While to date there are no good examples of truly integrated systems that are operating effectively, Cohen and Ooms (1993) note that "the new wave of complex, family-centered, more integrated services is forcing the field to rethink its methodology and emphasizes the importance of improving basic data systems."

- *Nonprofit organizations should be willing to collect, manage, and disseminate information that will allow them to fully participate in this rethinking of evaluation and information management.* Otherwise, nonprofit leaders could well see their role in theory building usurped by people who lack real-world experience in service delivery.

Example: Community Health Worker (CHW) programs use lay community advisers to promote health care in their own communities. Their techniques include nonmedical education, advocacy, social and psychological support, risk identification, case management, and treatment monitoring in homes and community meetings. CHW programs depend on a high degree of trust between workers and their respective communities, the development of which often requires several years. Due in large part to a lack of credible evaluation information, CHW programs have struggled to attract enough funding to become institutionalized in U.S. health care systems. Good evaluation information would allow CHW programs to build a conceptual and theoretical model that demonstrates to key stakeholders the need for funding beyond the usual two to three years of support that most funders are willing to provide. It would also allow for the identification of evaluation indicators that are appropriate for the CHW field. The development of grounded theory and appropriate evaluation indicators will require the full involvement of CHW practitioners, if both theory and indicators are to reflect the realities of the field.

ELEMENTS OF MANAGEMENT INFORMATION SYSTEMS

The examples described in previous sections demonstrate that management information systems serve multiple purposes and come in a variety of shapes and sizes depending on the needs and capacities of the organizations they serve. The phrase "form follows function" is especially appropriate for MIS, since the information needs of key stakeholders—not the technology available—should determine the system design. We cannot overemphasize that MIS are most powerful when they respond to the *specific* interests of stakeholders:

- Who are the relevant stakeholders (including you)?
- What information do they want?
- What information will have the greatest impact on the organization?
- What vehicles will best communicate this information?

Answers to these questions should drive the development of MIS.

Despite the variations in MIS from organization to organization, we believe a number of elements are essential to effective information management. Our experience with nonprofit organizations, private foundations, and state and federal agencies also suggests that some of the most critical—yet most basic—elements are often the most overlooked.

- *Organizational culture that values information:* The single most important step in developing a management information system is to make it an integral part of the organizational culture. Regardless of the organization's size, information management needs to permeate the very essence of the organization—from volunteers to paid staff to board members. It must be the responsibility of everyone in the organization, and therefore must be reflected in the organization's formal and informal reward systems. Evaluation, and the use of the information it yields, should be taken very seriously.

• *Time to reflect:* Anyone who has ever been involved with a nonprofit organization recognizes the scarcity and value of time. Unfortunately, the pressure to deliver services often leaves little time to reflect on whether those services could be improved. Successful organizations do not leave opportunities for reflection on evaluation information to pure chance, nor do they relegate reflection exclusively to upper-level administrators. Rather, they find the time for everyone in the organization to grapple with the meaning and implications of information collected during the evaluation process. Reflection is the core of information management.

• *Stakeholder identification:* Critics of MIS often argue that organizations suffer not from a lack of information, but from an overabundance of it. We have found this perception to be true only in those organizations that have not taken the time to identify the information needs of their key stakeholders. Management information systems that make use of stakeholder identification allow nonprofit organizations to concentrate their energies on information that is truly useful. Information that is not useful is disregarded, while useful information is shared with those who need it, when it is needed, and in the best format.

• *Asking good questions:* Directly related to stakeholder identification is the task of asking the right questions. What do stakeholders want to know, why do they want to know it, when do they need it, and what is the best vehicle for providing it? Answers to these four questions allow organizations to design systems that produce usable information instead of data factories that churn out reams of paper no one will ever read.

• *Comfort with incomplete data:* Information management is not an end in itself, but rather a tool that must be immediately available when nonprofit leaders make decisions. As cluster evaluator Rebecca Henry (1996) points out, "Decision makers cannot wait for the perfect data set: evaluators who seek to provide it may be left behind as program leaders move on to the next issue. Timing is everything." Effective organizations recognize that providing incomplete information in a timely fashion to decision makers is better than providing complete information after the fact.

• *Communications calendar:* Information use needs to be more than a random event. Many nonprofit leaders find it helpful to plan a communication strategy at least one year in advance, timing the release of information to annual campaigns, membership meetings, and other major events. The most basic form of communications calendar is a "tickler file" that reminds staff members of important deadlines. Like many of the elements of MIS, the development of communication strategies must be linked back to the information needs of stakeholders.

- *Employee, board, and volunteer orientation:* Successful nonprofit organizations make certain that people who are new to the organization understand and embrace its history, as well as its quest for continuous improvement. Board notebooks, orientation meetings, and retreats are excellent opportunities to pass along information that not only improves people's effectiveness in their own roles, but also demonstrates the organization's commitment to information use.

- *Board minutes, organizational histories, and other records of decisions:* A surprising number of nonprofit organizations fail to keep basic records of important decisions. Not only does this leave the organization vulnerable to potential legal trouble, it also does a disservice to employees, board members, and volunteers who want to understand why things are the way they are. Organizations that record important decisions and the reasons behind them are able to avoid perpetual struggles with the same issues.

- *Fund raising plans and donor information:* Despite all the attention devoted to the role of the federal government and private foundations in providing financial support for the nonprofit sector, donations from individuals still represent the majority of funding for most organizations. Yet most people in a community are never asked to donate to a nonprofit organization other than their church. Even more surprising, many first-time donors are never asked to make a second donation. MIS can play a critical role in identifying, cultivating, and nurturing donors.

- *Backup records:* Accidents happen. Employees accidentally erase computer files. Buildings burn. Information that is worth keeping in the first place is worth backing up from time to time. Off-site storage of copies of critical information is also recommended.

- *Confidentiality:* Nonprofit organizations must take every precaution to respect the confidences of clients, employees, and donors. This involves limiting access to certain types of information—by locking file cabinets in low-tech systems, or by requiring user identification codes and passwords for gaining entry to electronic information in more advanced systems. Organizations should also have an informed consent process that allows clients, staff, and donors to give written permission for the release of information.

OVERCOMING BARRIERS TO INFORMATION MANAGEMENT

Despite the many benefits of information management, there are a number of perceptual barriers that prevent the full implementation of effective systems. The first and most important step in overcoming these perceptual barriers is to recognize them as the myths they are. For example:

- *Perception:* Management information systems require major investments of time and money that are beyond the reach of most nonprofit organizations.

Reality: The effective management of information *does* require an investment of time. However, like any good investment it pays dividends in the long run. Fostering this attitude at the upper levels of an organization allows an information mind-set to permeate the entire organization. And as several examples in this chapter demonstrate, MIS need not cost a great deal.

- *Perception:* Nonprofit organizations lack the technical capacity to implement management information systems.

Reality: Information use—not technology—should drive the design of MIS. The most important capacity required to implement MIS is the ability to ask good questions and make the answers available to the people who need them.

- *Perception:* MIS reveals damaging information that can jeopardize the future of the organization.

Reality: All organizations can be more effective than they currently are. The organizations that run the greatest risk of extinction are the ones that fail to gather the information they need to make needed improvements. MIS will not jeopardize your organization's future—it will help ensure it.

SUMMARY

This chapter demonstrates that information is a critical tool in the management of nonprofit organizations. Good information allows organizations to improve their services, to plan for the future by learning from the past, to remain true to their missions, and to demonstrate their worth to key stakeholders. Information management also allows community-based organizations to play a major role in the design, conduct, and evaluation of complex initiatives aimed at effecting changes in social systems and policy at the state and federal levels.

Management information systems are the procedures used to collect, record, store, retrieve, tabulate, and report data. Information management is a process, a way of thinking that emphasizes the value and power of good information. As long as an organization focuses on the uses of information rather than on the means of managing it, MIS can be as complex as a computer system or as simple as a filing cabinet. The best systems are those that are commensurate with the ability of organizations to manage them.

References

Buhl, L. C. "The Evaluation Paradox." *Foundation News and Commentary,* Jan.-Feb. 1996, pp. 35–37.

Cohen, E., and Ooms, T. *Data Integration and Evaluation: Essential Components of Family-Centered Systems Reform.* Washington, D.C.: Family Impact Seminar, 1993.

Gray, S. T. (ed.). *A Vision of Evaluation.* Washington, D.C.: INDEPENDENT SECTOR, 1993.

Henry, R. C. "Evaluation as a Tool for Reform." In R. W. Richards (ed.), *Building Partnerships: Educating Health Professionals for the Communities They Serve.* San Francisco: Jossey-Bass, 1996.

Sanders, J. R. "Uses of Evaluation as a Means Toward Organizational Effectiveness." In S. T. Gray (ed.), *A Vision of Evaluation.* Washington, D.C.: INDEPENDENT SECTOR, 1993.

CHAPTER TEN

Resource Development

Peter McE. Buchanan
Theodore P. Hurwitz

There are at least four major approaches to the use of evaluation in the charitable community that could, if used in concert, dramatically improve resource development in the United States. Given the ever-increasing demand for their services, U.S. nonprofits need to pay close attention to any activity that stands to enhance their fund raising efforts.

First, evaluation must become an ongoing process used throughout the organization by staff and volunteers in a disciplined, systematic way. That ongoing process, tailor-made to the institution, consists of asking relevant questions, gathering the information necessary to answer them, and sharing the results with all parties so that organizational decisions about resource development are based on appropriate information.

Second, the focus of evaluation must be on the process of resource development, not just the results. The amount of money coming in at the moment can fluctuate for many reasons, so it is important to look at the fund raising process itself in good times as well as bad. Improving the process will lead to a long-term upward trend that will override any short-term setbacks.

Third, the nonprofit community must adopt the discipline and accountability of a business approach to resource development. Business process management adapts as well to effectiveness, efficiency, and adaptability in nonprofit resource development as to marketing in the for-profit world.

And finally, resource development must be included in any current efforts to set institutional performance benchmarks. Even where the percentage of the budget provided by fund raising is small, the work done with those funds is important to its beneficiaries. Paying attention to resource development is the best way to make sure that it continues to grow.

The organization that focuses only on evaluating results will inevitably handicap the future potential of its resource development. Resource development in any nonprofit organization is a critical indicator of the importance of a nonprofit organization's mission and the effectiveness with which that mission is pursued, but the incoming resource stream—even coupled with the composition of the donor population at any given moment—is not necessarily a reliable indicator of the quality of the resource development effort from one period to the next.

MAKING SURE THE PROCESS IS RIGHT

Over and above the ongoing, day-to-day evaluation discussed elsewhere in this volume, an annual self-evaluation is a most important step in resource development. A nonprofit should evaluate itself at least once every year, during the time the organization presents its traditional report on outcomes to volunteers, boards, charitable organizations, and the public at large. An annual evaluation is prudent, and it also makes sense from the standpoint of public relations and fund raising.

The only way such an evaluation can be soundly constructed is through the creation of monthly, or at least quarterly, measurements of performance against similar past periods of time. Here are some examples of such measurements:

- Dollar value and numbers of public and private cash commitments received.
- Dollar value and numbers of public and private gifts received and pledges.
- Dollar value and numbers of public and private proposals that are pending with grantors or prospective donors.
- Dollar value and numbers of proposals in preparation for funders' consideration.
- Percent of submitted proposals funded.
- Dollar value and numbers of all of the preceding categories by grant (or gift) sizes.
- Dollar value and numbers of all of the above categories by donor types

(trustees, state agencies, alumni, major donors, annual giving donors, foundations, corporations, and so on).

- Number of in-person fund raising calls.
- Number of grantor and donor prospects by dollar potential on file.
- Donor retention rate.
- Number of volunteer leaders recruited by type of activity (directors and trustees, fund raising volunteers, government contact committee members, and so on).
- Financial progress against critical organizational funding priorities established by the board.
- Measurement of the timeliness and the number of gift and grant acknowledgments to donors.
- Cost of resource development over time, as compared to peer institutions' experience and as a percentage of total dollars received by the organization.

When an organization reports these types of private and public fund raising results to its board, it should accompany the figures with a thoughtful evaluation of at least the following crucial resource development process components. Some are self-explanatory; others will receive more comment later in the chapter.

- Is our mission clearly articulated and compelling in purpose?
- Does our board have the capacity as well as the demonstrated commitment to giving it should have?
- How strong is our volunteer management, communication, and stewardship?
- Is the chief executive officer an effective resource developer?
- How effective is our staff leadership of resource development?
- How has each resource development program performed qualitatively?
- Is the resource development budget adequate?
- How effective is the fiscal management of the organization as a whole?

While considering these components, it is useful to note Susan Axelrod's set of complementary questions that charitable organizations seldom or never ask of themselves: "What would the world be without your program? Are you here to stay? Is your mission valued by today's potential donors? Does it have a broad-based appeal? Do your programs make a difference in today's society?" (1994, p. 36). These are important questions to consider.

But realistically speaking, few will ask these questions except within an overall study by a management consultant or a trustee who is not under the control of management. That is why the role of the board is so important in evaluation. In the very best organizations, governing boards not only prepare job descriptions for each board position but also use those criteria to evaluate each board member's performance. In the resource development field, probably the organizations that do this best are sophisticated foundations whose primary purpose is to develop private resources for publicly funded institutions. (The Indiana University Foundation Board provides an example of this kind of evaluation. For more information, write to Curtis R. Simic, President, Indiana University Foundation, P.O. Box 500, Bloomington, IN 47402.) The number of charitable organizations that follow this practice is unknown, but it probably totals fewer than a thousand of the more than three hundred thousand charitable organizations in the United States. Nevertheless, those that evaluate themselves stand as models of the appropriate governing board—and, parenthetically, chief executive officer—that many charitable organizations would do well to adopt.

Another important component to consider is volunteer engagement. According to INDEPENDENT SECTOR's 1994 findings, volunteer participation is sharply down in the United States. This is despite the fact that studies of the factors that are vital to successful resource development point again and again to the importance of volunteer involvement (*Giving and Volunteering*, 1995, p. 3).

But how many charitable organizations assess the strength of their volunteer organizations at least annually? Because it costs so little to ask for volunteers' opinions of how well they are being used to fulfill the organization's mission, all organizations should conduct such assessments and then use them to their advantage.

There are many ways to do this. The organization can mail out a postcard survey, arrange focus groups with volunteers before a meeting, or conduct a randomized set of brief telephone interviews. Any of these can yield invaluable insights into volunteer strength and how it can become even stronger. The findings are vitally important, but so is the fact that the organization is seeking the advice of volunteers and not simply asking them to assume another task.

In this context, the single most important and yet most overlooked component of volunteer communication is stewardship. Thanking volunteers for their time, talent, and treasure is one of the most powerful means of strengthening volunteer activity, and yet it is often an afterthought or woefully underbudgeted, or both! The strength of volunteer involvement in society depends on a marked improvement in the simple but essential business of consistently saying "Thank you."

Staff leadership of resource development is an area that has suffered from a lack of evaluation for a variety of reasons, among which are benign and purposeful neglect. Because staff evaluations have been driven almost solely by short-term results, such evaluations have been brief and often incomplete or unfair. For example, if an institution's annual giving program is in a modest decline but overall gift receipts are ahead of the year's targets, the staff director may well receive a vote of confidence regardless of the longer-term implications. Most charitable organizations rarely do program-by-program evaluation at the senior level. Often staff leadership is based on short-term results, and this is a mistake. Management must turn to multiple long-term measures of staff leadership to improve resource development.

Staff leaders should be accountable for program-by-program evaluation and should present those evaluations at the highest levels, especially to the members of the governing board. That responsibility would ensure a better understanding of resource development and how to make it more effective. A corollary benefit would be a far more sophisticated evaluation of all those involved and their responsibilities in each aspect of the resources program.

Finally, the adequacy of resource development budgets needs special consideration. This has been one of the most controversial areas in charitable activity, principally because of the arguments alluded to earlier about the cost of fund raising and the difficulty of agreeing on the true potential of any given institution. In most circumstances, these difficulties are allowed to preclude a serious discussion of whether, in principle and on the merits, more or less funding should be devoted to resource development. Today there is a growing body of data and sophisticated analyses that many institutions can use as the basis for a serious discussion of budget adequacy.

A further aspect of this component of resource development deserves comment. Rarely does anyone discuss budget adequacy outside the general budget parameters of the charity as a whole. While it may be inappropriate to finance resource development outside those parameters, failing to consider doing so is an obvious shortcoming in any evaluation of resource development. The current attitude is that resource development must "do more with less" because that is the general economic outlook for the charitable community as a whole. While that may be accurate, investing less in resource development may be one of the worst things charities can do in such an environment. Budget adequacy is a vital part of resource development evaluation; it cannot continue to be ignored. But needless to say, it is almost impossible for staff to take the initiative on this issue, which is why recognition of the importance of budget must come from the board and chief executive officer.

Together, all these critical components of successful resource development should be evaluated along with traditional results. Such a change would encourage a more comprehensive approach to evaluation and place the focus on the process as a whole, not just short-term results.

TAKING A BUSINESSLIKE APPROACH

The third recommended change in evaluation is to be more businesslike. We should take full advantage of the enormous strides the business community has made in process management, which has significantly raised the quality of goods and services and the level of customer satisfaction over the past twenty-five years. The three broad purposes of business process management—effectiveness, efficiency, and adaptability—are as applicable to resource development in the charitable community as to marketing in the business community. To deny the parallels is to forsake an enormous opportunity for gains in performance.

Process management involves three main steps: to define the core processes of the organization or of a particular function of the organization; to measure how effective, efficient, and adaptable those processes are; and finally to compare those measurements against comparable world standards to determine how those processes can be improved. Evaluation then becomes a continuous cycle of self-improvement.

James Greenfield describes the application of these principles to resource development, at least in part, in a 1995 paper titled "Cost and Performance Measurements." In it, he argues that any nonprofit can develop performance measurements that will, over a three-year period, "demonstrate effectiveness, efficiency, productivity, and profitability in resource development" (p. 5). The performance measures he recommends are generally obtainable: number of participants, income received, expense incurred, percent participation, average gift size, net income, average cost per gift, cost-effectiveness, and return on investment. Hence, any charitable organization with computerized gift information and the ability to manipulate it can come up with those measures for each of its different solicitation programs. Once the data are gathered, it is then up to each organization to determine what it can achieve and if it can "measure up."

If evaluation is to become the powerful tool it should be to improve performance, staff leaders of resource development programs must avail themselves of these measurements. Governing board members have both a right to know this information and a responsibility for knowing it. In fact, resource development is one of the three primary responsibilities that a governing board cannot delegate (Howe, 1991, p. 3). As a result, no matter how true it is that fund raising is a process of building long-term relationships, measuring the performance of fund raising activities is absolutely essential to evaluate fairly their value and potential. Every chief executive officer has a special responsibility to see that staff members take these and other performance measures frequently and consistently so that they can continually improve.

In addition to the interest scholars have shown in performance measures, three leading international organizations have also been working on benchmarking as part of their commitment to performance and accountability in resource development. The Council for Advancement and Support of Education (CASE), the National Society of Fund Raising Executives (NSFRE), and the Association for Healthcare Philanthropy (AHP) have worked independently and cooperatively to further develop measures of performance. Several examples of work supported by them are included in the reference material for this chapter; see Costa (1994), a professional paper describing reports and formulas to use in measuring the effectiveness and productivity of health care fund raising programs, and also National Society of Fund Raising Executives (1994) and Council for Advancement and Support of Education (1995).

No matter how important these performance measures are, business process management extends well beyond them into every aspect of an organization's life. It concentrates on the core and subcore processes that drive an organization to achieve those outcomes. It is in this area that the nonprofit community generally has little if any experience. If the results discussed earlier depend on how effectively the major gifts officers conduct their work, then business process management seeks to define their key processes, measure them, and then constantly compare them with others to see how to improve them.

For example, if a critical core process for a major gifts officer is to match donor prospects and institutional needs, how does that process work? What is in the process, what is not in it, what input is necessary to gain the output, who provides that input, how timely is it, and how do we measure its effectiveness and its efficiency? If the major gifts officer can dramatically improve the effectiveness of matching donors and institutional needs, is there any doubt that the fund raising outcomes will eventually improve also?

Another example of a critical core process is the identification of new qualified prospects. If the process of identification can be significantly improved, there should eventually be better resource development performance because new prospects can be solicited as effectively in less time.

Such approaches to core processes have transformed some businesses. Although there are differences between businesses and charities, there is no reason to believe process management cannot also transform resource development in the charitable community.

Finally, resource development should become an integral part of the overall performance measures for institutions as a whole. Even when resource development accounts only for a small percentage of institutional income, it usually provides a significant substantive benefit to its beneficiaries and is viewed by the public at large as a reflection of its strength and future prospects.

It was little more than a decade ago that at least one Ivy League campus questioned the importance of publishing its fund raising results in its annual report. That reflected then and speaks now to the overall power of evaluation. If a charity does not believe its resource development is important enough to merit publishing as one of its measures of long-term health, that program is unlikely to spawn the kind of evaluative process that will ensure improved performance year after year.

TAKING RESPONSIBILITY
FOR RESULTS

There is another less compelling but nevertheless real reason to be proactive about including resource development performance in overall institutional measurements. The reason is that if charitable institutions do not choose to do so, someone else may do it for them. Witness *U.S. News and World Report*'s annual "America's Best Colleges," which allots 5 percent of its national ranking to the average percentage of undergraduate alumni who give to the college. As one experienced college advancement vice president noted, "Average net operating support per alumnus over a six-year period is the most accurate figure to demonstrate how successfully the college raises dollars from its constituents" (Lowery, 1995, p. 1). *U.S. News and World Report* is always willing to discuss its ratings, but the magazine is hardly likely to change this particular formula after years of great commercial success.

In searching for new keys to evaluating resource development, we believe first that timely—hopefully monthly—and consistent measurements of performance provide the only certain foundation for successful evaluation. It is vitally important to then move from results evaluation to process evaluation if the organization is to capitalize on that foundation. Third, we feel that business process management not only furthers that conceptual commitment but also drives continuous improvements in the way resource development functions on a daily basis. An important characteristic of business process management is empowering each individual in the organization to make those improvements as opportunities arise. Finally, we believe resource development must be publicly acknowledged as a key measure of institutional health. Together, these four steps will encourage good questions that few nonprofit organizations are asking, secure new information from every corner of the organization, and provide the basis for better decision making. In addition, it will raise all our constituents' consciousness of issues that affect our organizations. Indeed, that may be the most important result of the entire evaluation process.

References

Axelrod, S. L. "Building a Development Operation: Are You Really Ready for It?" *Fund Raising Management,* 1994, *26*(12), 36.

Costa, N. G. *Measuring Progress and Success in Fund Raising.* Falls Church, Va.: Association for Healthcare Philanthropy, 1994.

Council for Advancement and Support of Education. *Institutional Outcomes Measures Survey.* Commission on Alumni Relations, Alumni Support Index Project, 1995.

Giving and Volunteering in the United States, 1994, Vol. 2. Washington, D.C.: INDEPENDENT SECTOR, 1995.

Greenfield, J. M. "Cost and Performance Measurements." Paper presented at the NSFRE Research Council's 1995 Think Tank on Fund Raising Research at Indiana University, June 1–3, 1995.

Howe, F. *The Board Member's Guide to Fund Raising: What Every Trustee Needs to Know About Raising Money.* San Francisco: Jossey-Bass, 1991.

Lowery, W. R. "Benchmarks for Comparison: Hearty Colleges and Other Small Liberal Arts Colleges." Paper submitted to the Council for Advancement and Support of Education, Fall 1995.

National Society of Fund Raising Executives. *Guidelines Useful to Not-for-Profit Organizations for Evaluating the Appropriateness of Their Fund Raising Costs.* Alexandria, Va.: National Society of Fund Raising Executives, 1994.

CHAPTER ELEVEN

Ethics and Accountability

Judy Belk
Michael Daigneault

Leaders in the nonprofit and foundation communities plow a field filled with ethical land mines no less perilous than ones navigated by the corporate and government sectors of our economy. Nonetheless, many nonprofit leaders ignore organizational ethics as a management imperative. This is so even though those very same leaders are instrumental in shaping their organization's culture, and a number of independent sector organizations have come under scrutiny for various business practices.

We have organized our discussion of some of the more important ethical issues facing the independent sector into a series of key questions that lend themselves to a process of continuous evaluation and renewal. Each of these key questions, in turn, causes us to ask a number of follow-up questions that will assist your organization in evaluating its own ethics and accountability on an ongoing basis.

ETHICAL CHOICES

Our discussion begins with a fundamental question, the reverse of the more traditional question of why individuals we would consider to be "bad" make improper or unethical choices. The really critical question facing most individuals and organizations in the independent sector (as elsewhere) is

Why do good people sometimes make bad ethical choices?

As long as I hire good people, a nonprofit leader might assume, I'll minimize ethical lapses. Organizations, like people, generally have good intentions; they want to do the right thing—want to be perceived as fair, as compassionate, and as providing high-quality services to clients or customers. But even employees and organizations of sound moral fiber have been known to falter.

Good people often make bad ethical choices based on any number of the following types of rationalizations or pressures:

- What we're doing isn't *really* unethical or illegal. . . .
- We have to cut some corners to get the job done. . . .
- We've got to do something drastic—there's no time (or money) to take the long way around. . . .
- Everybody else is doing it. . . .
- It's safe; we'll never get caught. . . .
- It's in a good cause, so it's OK. . . .
- You've got to look out for yourself. . . .

Other factors can lead well-intentioned people to make bad decisions. Many convince themselves that because the activity or decision appears to help their organization, the organization would condone it and even reward the person who engages in the behavior. Some organizations reduce the quality of their internal decision making by applying incessant pressure to produce and by focusing only on results and the bottom line. Bad decisions also sometimes emerge from efforts to respond to conflicting interests of competing stakeholders and also simply from fear.

For men and women of good conscience, ethical choices may appear pretty clear-cut in the abstract. Few readers will have had much patience for the listed rationalizations, separated as they were from issues that would make them make sense "just this once." However, the ethical waters we wade into are often rather murky. They involve ethical and nonethical values at odds with each other and various outcomes that often affect multiple stakeholders.

Some organizations are involved in ongoing dialogues with their employees about tackling ethical challenges and creating a risk-free environment that encourages open debate. But achieving a comfort level that allows employees to speak openly requires thoughtful design, according to Michael Rion, author of *The Responsible Manager* (1996). As Rion points out, there is no guarantee that providing structure for ethical dialogues will protect employees from threats, retaliation, or job loss.

One way an organization can display its commitment to ethical behavior is by involving upper management in ethical dialogues. When employees see that upper management is investing its time in such an endeavor, that pursuit of a higher moral conscience will most likely spread throughout the organization.

Fostering an ongoing dialogue with employees can help to direct them toward specific ethical codes or guidelines, instruct them on when to trust their own judgment and when to report others (vendors, fellow employees, clients, or other stakeholders) whose behavior may be questionable. An organization might consider establishing an anonymous channel for those reluctant to step forward. It is not enough to define ethical behavior and hope that ethical transgressions will not occur; people must see that the organization disciplines ethical transgressions and does not condone them.

To take an example from the for-profit realm, the mission of Levi Strauss & Company is clear: the apparel manufacturer is dedicated to "responsible commercial success as a global marketing company" that conducts business "ethically" while demonstrating "leadership in satisfying responsibilities to our communities and to society."

Levi Strauss provides further evidence of the company's achievement in devising a six-part aspirations statement that espouses such values as teamwork and trust, communications, empowerment, and ethical management.

As Chairman and Chief Executive Officer Robert Haas indicates, the ultimate test of a company's mission is reflected in employee decisions:

"The future is not going to be shaped by me or even by the aspirations statement," Haas states. "It's going to be shaped by our people and their actions, by the questions they ask and the responses we give, and by how this feeds into the way we run our business."

Organizations like Levi Strauss must address critical values questions that include

- Assessing aspirational values and operational values.
- Determining whether those values differ.
- Encouraging individuals within an organization to question whether their personal values are aligned with the organization's values.

Nonprofits and Ethical Conduct

Today's climate of economic globalization and competition, combined with more vigilant media and tougher legal standards, makes it necessary for nonprofit leaders to redefine and focus on ethical conduct in the hope of improving their organizations' reputation. Whether an organization succeeds in its mission may well be contingent upon establishing and maintaining both the reality and the image of ethical conduct.

Once an organization commits to a set of ethical expectations, its leaders must realize that ethics is not a one-stop measure. Rather, it is a journey, and a bumpy one at times. It is not enough to adopt a code of ethics, tender it to employees, and presume that they will act accordingly. (Nor is it sufficient to devise a compliance-based program that emphasizes penalties. Whereas compliance policies most often seek to prevent criminal misconduct, a broader ethics program encourages responsible conduct. An emphasis on both compliance and ethics is needed to create a mature and successful program.)

Organizations with an eye toward integrity must undertake a comprehensive approach that goes well beyond a written code or an array of sanctions for misdeeds. Only when an organization's top-level officials acknowledge ethics as indispensable is it likely to permeate every level of an operation, as Johnson & Johnson illustrated when it moved in 1982 to recall Tylenol from pharmacy shelves nationwide.

The Tylenol Recall

James Burke, Johnson & Johnson's chief operating officer at the time, often receives a good deal of credit for orchestrating the recall after seven people died as a result of product tampering at the point of sale. Yet the recall could not have been executed without cooperation from employees at various levels. Success was more a matter of overall approach than of one executive's moral conviction.

Johnson & Johnson had mapped out its organizational culture long before the Tylenol crisis. Armed with that foresight, Burke was able to steer the company capably through a stormy period. Johnson & Johnson must have regarded the side benefits of proper conduct early on, acknowledging integrity as a necessary component of employee values, the foundation on which to build a sound reputation and a means of heightening a public trust. It worked.

But how did Johnson & Johnson become an ethical paragon? We will explore the components of organizational integrity that not only exemplify the corporate ethos that permitted Johnson & Johnson to emerge successfully from the Tylenol incident but also that should be exhibited by nonprofit organizations that are equally challenged to devise ethics programs and policies.

ORGANIZATIONAL INTEGRITY

In ethics as in every area of organizational life, success requires asking good questions, collecting the information, and sharing and using that information to inform good decisions. Organizations don't fall accidentally into an ethical stance. As we've discussed, no matter how good the intentions of the organization as a whole and the people working in it, the pressure to trim and cut corners and make defensive choices is constant. The questions raised here will open a discussion aimed at combating that pressure.

Values

What are our organization's values?

"To preserve and advance its mission is central to an organization's integrity," states Robert Lawry, director of the Center for Professional Ethics at Case Western Reserve University in Cleveland, Ohio. The mission of a nonprofit or charitable organization must, therefore, be clearly defined. Flowing from its mission statement, each nonprofit organization applies a set of values to carry out its mission. These values may be stated in a formal code or credo or may be unwritten and even unconscious. Whether conscious or unconscious, the values of your organization are crucial in furthering its mission and the specific goals designed to bring that mission into reality.

To carry out all actions regarding that mission, an organization must harmonize its mission and values. No matter what stage of development your organization may be in, asking yourself and other key stakeholders about what your organization's values are is an excellent place to start any inquiry concerning ethics and accountability.

Communication

Have we adequately communicated our organization's values internally and externally?

Once the values of an organization have been determined, it is essential to discover whether the efforts to communicate and reinforce such values throughout your stakeholder community have been successful.

One way of doing this is to ask your employees (and other stakeholders) to identify their core personal values. You can then ask them to articulate what they perceive to be your organization's values.

As part of this exercise, an organization's values can be roughly categorized in two ways: existent values and aspirational values. *Existent values* are those that are a current and predominant reality in your organization's culture. *Aspirational values* are those that your organization has articulated a desire to strive for but has not yet achieved to the degree that would make them existent values. In some cases like at Levi Strauss & Company, aspirational values denote an ongoing journey requiring investment and training and a recommitment to continually raising the bar. How do your organization's existent values differ (if at all) from what are perceived to be your organization's aspirational values?

In addition, key stakeholders (such as leadership, board, and staff) should be asked to compare their own values to those of your organization. Do their personal values differ from your organization's values, existent or aspirational?

Is there a large shift in values between management and other members of your staff? Is there a perception of a large gap between your organization's existent and aspirational values? Do your organization's existent values differ significantly from those of your employees? How about your donors? Or those to whom you give funds?

In general, the more in sync an individual's values are with those of the organization, the better. But the greater the divide, the more apt you are to question your organization's aims and encounter an ethical snare. Organizations can also consider whether they are adequately conveying their values by looking at the various methods that they communicate with their stakeholder community and assessing whether ethics and accountability is a vital part of the organization's message:

- Is ethics a factor in hiring, promotion, and termination decisions, distributing an organization's core values and ethical code to all new full-time and part-time employees?
- Is ethics a component of training for all incoming employees?
- Is ethics a component of the written communications flowing from your organization to your stakeholder community? Is it an important part of vital letters, memoranda, newsletters, annual reports, staff manuals, funding policies, and so on?
- Do you have a written ethics code or credo?
- Has staff had an opportunity to provide input into the credo or code?
- Are the ethical implications of decisions or policies openly talked about in board and staff meetings?
- Is ethical behavior a factor in performance reviews, promotions, and succession planning?

In general, the more an individual finds his or her values in sync with those of the organization, the better. But the greater the divide, the more apt you are to question your organization's aims and encounter an ethical snare.

Guidance

Have we established adequate ethics guidelines, policies, procedures, and management structure?

An organization may intend to promote ethical behavior, but it can do little to further its agenda without the proper management tools and structure. Not all organizations need the same set of tools but they should rely on some common features.

Does our organization have a written ethics guideline as in a credo or code?

An ethics credo is a brief set of aspirational principles articulating the values of your organization. A written code of ethics is a more comprehensive document that often incorporates the values in a credo into a more detailed set of rules, guidelines, definitions, penalties, and examples.

A code should be written in simple, straightforward terms, avoiding legalese as much as possible. Employees and other key stakeholders should find policies that govern how to treat an ethical complaint, what provisions exist to safeguard a complaint or complainant's confidentiality, and what penalties to impose for violating the code.

Do we have policies that further reinforce our organization's ethical principles, and have we harmonized such policies with our credo or code?

A critical task in any comprehensive ethics and accountability initiative is to ensure that the stated values and principles of the organization are actually being carried out according to the more detailed policies management articulates.

Do we have in place procedures that individuals can follow when asking an ethics question or reporting an ethics concern?

Do you have a designated ethics management and reporting structure? One of the most frequently overlooked features of an ethics and accountability program is the vital need for reporting or probing transgressions, such as an ethics committee of staff or board members, or an individual, such as a general counsel, to oversee those efforts. That committee or individual, in turn, needs direct access to an organization's top-level officials to lend credibility to the initiative and reinforce it as an organization's governing tenet.

Decision makers at all levels should be involved in the process of defining responsible and honest behavior, if that behavior is to be effective at all levels. Beyond that, an organization must integrate its policies into its day-to-day operations and harmonize its guiding values with its code of ethics.

An organization's general counsel can play a crucial role in achieving a successful ethics program by stimulating compliance with the law and fostering an ethical climate where individuals can be as successful, productive, and efficient as possible.

Ongoing ethics training is one necessary way to educate employees. Such training sessions can be led by managers or by ethics experts who can stimulate dialogue through focus groups, employee surveys, interactive workshops, seminars, videos, and written materials.

Accountability

To whom is our organization accountable?

Many people believe that charitable organizations do not face the same consequences for breaching ethical standards that those working in the government or for-profit sector confront. After all, nonprofit managers don't face reelection by the public and they don't have a bottom line that is as easy to analyze in terms of costs and profits. Yet the perception that charitable organizations are above reproach is not accurate; the nonprofit sector must answer to a number of stakeholders. Board members and top officials, legal rules and regulators, and a wary public are all driving forces of accountability.

The public particularly can serve as a nonprofit organization's most vigorous critic as well as its most stalwart advocate. That dual role exists for a number of reasons. For one thing, people expect nonprofits to be shrewder at spending than either government or commercial enterprises. They also view charitable organizations as role models for proper conduct. It follows, then, that people whom nonprofit groups solicit for support likewise will serve as watchdogs who rate organizations' performance and vilify any engaged in misconduct. Public disclosure constitutes an important accountability measure for charitable groups.

United Way Reunited

William Aramony, president of United Way of America, was convicted of charges of conspiracy, filing false income tax returns, and other misdeeds. Shortly after the scandal, United Way of America set out to construct an ethical framework that would safeguard against such ethical or financial abuses. But Charles Kolb, the organization's general counsel, insists that the new ethics programs—which began with a code of ethics in 1993—wasn't a chicken-egg evolution. "We didn't do this for the public perception," Kolb said. "We did it because it was the right thing to do. An ethical environment is part of the way a company should do business."

Nonprofit organizations could take a cue from United Way's ongoing strategy to promote ethical responsibility. After enacting the code, United Way sensitized staff at its national headquarters to the issues presented in the ethical code through training sessions and workshops provided by an outside ethics expert.

United Way repeats the workshops annually and introduces new employees to the code of ethics through meetings with the general counsel. A staff ethics committee and a board of trustees ethics committee oversee the integrity initiatives, assist in revising the code every two years, and review ethics complaints.

If public support erodes, so does an organization's capacity to serve the public. Individuals or leaders within an organization, then, are best served in making decisions when they pay attention to the ethical implications of their choices.

ETHICS AND SUCCESS

In today's Information Age, business ethics can no longer be dismissed as a fad of organizational management. Ethics is the cornerstone of a successful organization that uses core values to foster a climate of social and personal responsibility among its employees.

Although many organizations are embracing the trend to adopt codes of ethics, a code alone is not the solution. Indeed, a joint study of major U.S. companies by the Ethics Resource Center and the Behavior Research Center noted that organizations that consider their ethics programs successful possess, at a minimum, the following similarities:

- They follow a written code or credo that they distribute to all employees.
- They provide training that relates to their code and the code's application to everyday work situations. Such training takes a variety of forms.
- The credos and codes are reinforced constantly via videos, newsletter articles, posters, and talks by management.
- The organization has a process in place for holding every employee at every level accountable in ensuring that on-the-job behavior reflects the organization's ethical values.
- They maintain a regular pattern of monitoring and evaluating their codes and ethics programs.

Is ethics and accountability a leadership issue for your organization?
Nonprofit organizations must realize the importance of extending their ethical mission beyond their immediate circle so that their values are matched by vendors, organization members, customers, and other stakeholders. Such an approach creates a level playing field to develop policies and agreed-upon actions.

Above all, charitable organizations should subscribe to the concept of ethics as a tenet of leadership. In this case, the nonprofit sector should seize the opportunity to lead by example and to provide a guidepost of responsible and honest conduct through word and deed.

References

Chisolm, L. B. "Accountability of Nonprofit Management Organizations and Those Who Control Them: The Legal Framework." *Nonprofit Management and Leadership,* 1995, 6(2).

Ethics and the Nation's Voluntary and Philanthropic Community. Washington, D.C.: INDEPENDENT SECTOR, 1991.

Ethics, Inc. *United We Stand: Personal and Organizational Ethics in a New Era.* Falls Church, Va.: United Way of America, 1994.

Gray, S. T., and Stockdill, S. H. *Evaluation with Power.* Washington, D.C.: INDEPENDENT SECTOR, 1995.

Institute for Nonprofit Organization Management. *Ethics in Nonprofit Management.* San Francisco: College of Professional Studies, University of San Francisco, 1990.

Paine, L. S. "Managing for Organization Integrity." *Harvard Business Review,* Mar.-Apr. 1994.

Rion, M. *The Responsible Manager: Practical Strategies for Ethical Decision Making.* Amherst, Mass.: HRD Press, 1996.

CHAPTER TWELVE

Adapting the Evaluation Process to the Organizational Culture

Rebecca Adamson
Edward T. Weaver

The unique strength of ongoing evaluation is that it acknowledges that organizations differ one from the other, and that there is an internal and external context that influences and shapes each organization. Both the internal context (culture) and the external context (environment) change over time—organizations are not static entities subject to the same kind of analysis or evaluation a scientist would apply to a specimen on a microscope slide.

This chapter provides an extensive case study of one organization, First Nations Development Institute (FNDI), to show how ongoing evaluation can be adapted to a particular cultural context so as to enhance its purpose and not interfere with it. FNDI is a national Native American economic development organization working with tribes and Native people on the reservations to promote an economic environment that builds on local resources, recognizes Native knowledge and culture, and supports development from within communities. The organization defines its work as culturally appropriate, values-based development. It works at both the local community and the national levels to develop models and strategies that enhance Native peoples' control of their economic resources.

The case study is particularly useful because the concept of culture is an elusive one. Human shortcomings in finding words to define culture do not negate the existence of culture itself, as reflected in beliefs, behaviors, and symbols that have particular significance within organizations, groups, and societies.

BACKGROUND FROM THE LITERATURE

Despite the difficulty of defining culture, it is useful to explore the vocabulary that has been developed for the subject. Putnam (1993) uses a metaphor that helps give meaning to culture. He says it is the "symbolic soil" within which organizational processes take place. Others characterize culture as a blueprint for living or as social regularities (Kirkhart, 1995; Hughes, Seidman, and Williams, 1993).

Klitgaard (1995) defines sociocultural setting as "shared meanings, customary institutions, and something akin to a collective personality." Kirkhart (1995) expands the definition somewhat, drawing from several sources. She defines culture as "Common cultural experience, shared knowledge, stories, social definitions of language, customs, behaviors and artifacts" (p. 3). (See also Fine and Kleinman, 1979; Howard, 1991; Mair, 1988.) Kirkhart adds a particularly important perspective that "the most relevant questions may not be that of cultural membership but of strength of cultural commitments" (p. 3). The influence of culture on the individual or an organization is, therefore, dependent on the commitment or identification of the individual, organization, or group with the distinctive culture.

Schein (1992) synthesizes several definitions and adds his own perspective in his formal definition of culture. A group's culture, he says, can be defined as "a pattern of shared basic assumptions that the group learned as it solved its problems of external adaptation and internal integration, that has worked well enough to be considered valid and, therefore, to be taught to new members as the correct way to perceive, think, and feel in relation to those problems" (p. 12).

Schein's definition is helpful in that it derives from his differentiation among levels of culture. He identifies *artifacts* as the most visible and surface aspect of culture. Artifacts are very easy to observe and very difficult to interpret. The meaning in artifacts is to be found in an understanding of the underlying assumptions that define the culture. Artifacts are manifestations of the underlying assumptions. The second level is *espoused values,* which are reflected in the strategies, goals, and philosophies members of the group give voice to. The third level, at the heart of Schein's definition, is basic *underlying assumptions.* Basic underlying assumptions derive from repeated experience that confirms a value, belief, or hypothesis about what works and what is good. These basic assumptions frame what is acceptable behavior and what has meaning for the group. Behavior outside parameters framed by these assumptions is not understood, accepted, or considered rational (Schein, 1992, pp. 16–27).

Schein is working in the context of organizational culture and leadership. He views culture as perhaps the leader's most important responsibility—to understand it, to create it, and to change it as required for organizational effectiveness. His purpose then may influence his definition and view of group culture.

For example, he seems to be saying that culture is created or changed by a process that flows from symbols, artifacts, and language to espoused values, which may develop into values that guide behavior and then into the basic underlying assumptions—the essence of culture—that are taken for granted almost, if not actually, at a subconscious level. On the other hand, an alternative conceptualization that could be equally compelling is that basic underlying assumptions are the foundation for values, and for artifacts, symbols, language, and other visible manifestations of culture. The latter assumption seems to apply more closely to the case study in this chapter than does Schein's "managed" approach, but Schein's work remains valuable in its own context. He is specifically dealing with the leader's role in culture formation and change, which, by definition, is a more intentional and managed process than that undertaken by FNDI, which is working to preserve and maintain a strong culture already in existence.

Several useful observations can be drawn from these attempts to define the somewhat ambiguous concept of culture. First, the implications of culture on various group and organizational processes is relatively unexplored. That is particularly so with respect to evaluation design, implementation, and interpretation. Second, the symbols, artifacts, language, and espoused values of a group or organization do not define the essence of the culture. They are only clues, indicators of the essence of culture—and very misleading ones at times. "The map is not the territory" is an appropriate expression in making this point. The territory of a culture is its basic underlying assumptions, which are often very difficult to identify—but anything short of those assumptions are only representations of culture. Nevertheless, artifacts and values offer clues that may be very helpful in opening doors to the essence of the group culture.

Further, when basic underlying assumptions are identified, Kirkhart's observation that cultural membership is not the same as strength of cultural commitment takes on a deeper meaning. It is commitment to the basic underlying assumptions that makes for ownership of a culture. Participating in rituals or espousing values does not necessarily indicate commitment. Some of us, perhaps, have shallow, transient, and very changing cultural commitment. It is therefore not within our experience or understanding to fathom the significance of enduring cultural commitment that we encounter in other groups or organizations. Native Americans, for example, increasingly examine behaviors, opportunities, and organizational processes as to their "cultural appropriateness." Many of us, who understand the world in which we live as structured, technical, and to a large degree mechanical, are not sure what "cultural appropriateness" means to us—and therefore we find it very difficult to comprehend what it may mean to Native people.

Another caution, or question, should be raised when interpreting or ascribing certain characteristics to a *culture.* Looking forward to the case study as an example of evaluation that seeks to take culture into account, we can ask whether there is a single Native American culture. Or are there many different cultures and subcultures, within which there may be some common threads? If, indeed, it is perilous to generalize, evaluators will need to be careful to tune in to the nuances of the particular program, organization, or subpart of an organization with which they are working. It is likely that the actual implementation of an initiative will incorporate the values and objectives of the particular implementing group. Such cultural influences may be within the funder's conception of "project objectives," or such influences may, at times, be inconsistent with project objectives.

This possible dichotomy points to the importance of early exploration of the purposes of programs or organizations to ensure that they are culturally appropriate. It is our premise that evaluation that does not take into account the unique culture of each organization (or program) runs a significant risk of framing the questions in a less than optimal way, of employing methodologies that generate weak data, and lose or misinterpret the meaning of the data.

The case study illustrates both evaluation that seeks to take culture into account and an application of the vision of evaluation that focuses on learning and improvement as a way to achieve organization and program effectiveness and desirable outcomes. It is an approach that values selecting and using methodologies that serve the stakeholders' objectives rather than attempting to make the purposes and objectives of the organization and its stakeholders fit a set of evaluation models and techniques.

FIRST NATIONS DEVELOPMENT INSTITUTE: A CASE STUDY

During its sixteen years in Native American community and systemic reform, FNDI determined that state-of-the-art evaluations for economic development programs had little to do with social change, social or environmental costs, or specific cultural differences. Invariably, economic indicators focused only on what could be definitively quantified. Therefore, for FNDI to try and adapt any outside evaluation framework would result in a huge gap between what was measured and the mission and cultural underpinning of FNDI and how people defined success.

Recognizing the importance of culture and values and the limitations of standard, traditional evaluation forms, FNDI sought to develop a framework that takes culture into account. With support from the Joyce and Levi Strauss Foundations, FNDI developed the "Elements of Development" framework, also called the "Development Wheel," which is shown in Figure 12.1.

The Elements of Development framework allows for the combination of traditional Western measurements of finite numbers and other evaluative features with the more holistic and elusive indicators associated with personal or organizational development or growth of a community. The elements, which emanate from four integral points—control of assets, kinship, personal efficacy, and spirituality—form a circle. The circle is a sacred symbol to Native peoples, representing the balance and interconnectedness among all areas of life. It is used to demonstrate a holistic model by visually indicating that one cannot look at parts of the whole, but must see the entire picture. Evaluations that focus on one quadrant of the circle—say, "control of assets"—and ignore other aspects of the program and organizational culture will never provide the energy that keeps an organization (or project) alive, vibrant, and dynamic.

The main axes of the circle represent major significant relationships:

- *Control of Assets:* The quality of the outcome—that is, service to Indian Country—is the uppermost consideration at FNDI. FNDI staff seek to work out a detailed process for best managing the available resources of time, talent, and money so as to ensure a high-quality outcome to any activity. The organization regards its staff as accountable to themselves, their constituencies, and their funders, and expects them to approach and complete their tasks accordingly.

- *Kinship:* Individuals and departments are parts of the larger whole whose functioning they can influence best by working together. They recognize a duty to respect one another in spite of any differences, responding on the basis of corporate values and decisions rather than individual moods and circumstances. FNDI expects them to act as positive representatives, and to share and celebrate successes, to acknowledge failure not to dwell on it but to learn from it and do better next time, and to adapt to inconveniences for the sake of a better outcome. Orderly cooperation is one key to success at FNDI.

- *Personal Efficacy:* FNDI expects its staff to focus on making things happen. They need to be confident enough to champion causes but self-correcting enough to learn from constructive criticism of individual performance. They should take pride in their work and therefore seek to increase knowledge and strive for excellence. They must be committed to their constituencies and take risks on their behalf. Self-enhancement and development are valued and encouraged and sub-par effort and performance are discouraged. "Testing the wing of the impossible," they seek to arouse potential within themselves and their constituents in Indian Country.

- *Spirituality:* FNDI expects its staff to value the unique position they hold in serving Indian people. They should strive to appreciate Native culture as a way of understanding Native people and the issues that affect them. They need to seek balance in their lives and recognize good humor as an important part of the mix. FNDI is preparing a better future for itself and Native people, and corporate spirituality plays a strong role in getting from the present to the future.

The FNDI view of evaluation goes beyond grading performance to focus on the development of Native people. Improvement and motivation come from

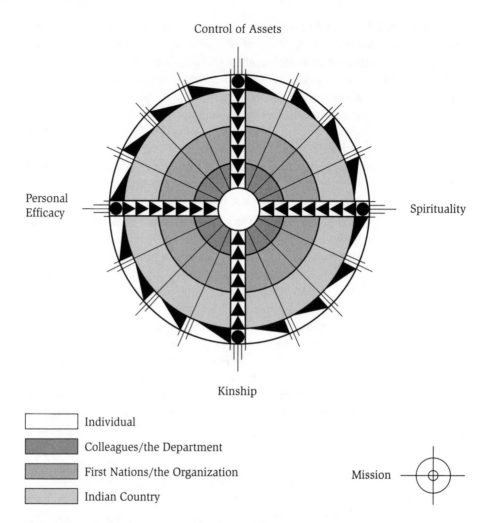

Figure 12.1. Evaluation Framework: The Development Wheel.

Source: Copyright © 1991 by First Nations Development Institute.

within. Development cannot be done *to* people or *for* people; it must come *from* people. A first step in empowerment is recognizing that personal values, belief systems, and traditional knowledge are valid and important. This is a crucial understanding within the organization's definition of ongoing evaluation. The evaluation framework is thus only a guide to be used by individuals, colleagues, and supervisors (in the case of staff evaluations) or by organizations (for self-evaluation or for specific projects) to develop their own measures and indicators of success and accomplishment. Within the four main quadrants, goals can be articulated and operating principles formulated that reflect the values and priorities of Native people.

To test the usefulness of the elements as a viable assessment tool, FNDI applied them to its own personnel evaluations. Subsequently, also based on this framework, FNDI and external consultants are assessing Eagle Staff Fund, FNDI's grant making and technical assistance project.

First Nations Staff Performance Evaluation

The staff evaluation process began at an informal breakfast gathering of four staff members and the president. The declared intention was not to launch an evaluation process, but to bring together a critical mass of high achievers within the office who could push and pull the organizational culture in the direction of steadily increasing high performance.

Regardless of stated plans, the initial meeting marked the beginning of what would become a distinct evaluation process. Although the elements framework had been designed with the intention of assessing community development, staff and the president decided to apply it toward developing indicators of staff performance.

Adapting the framework and developing a methodology appropriate to staff evaluations took eleven months (rather than the originally anticipated six), as organizational culture melded with an evaluation process. It took a full year to begin the actual staff evaluations.

To begin this process, FNDI adapted its principles of development to include the culture of the organization, the organization as a community, the people of the organization, and the organization mission—in other words, the synergy that connects FNDI to its greater purpose.

Relating to staff performance evaluations, the interior circle of the Development Wheel represents the individual. Starting from the smallest and moving outward, the expanding circles represent the individual, the department, the organization, and Native American interests, respectively. The circle exists within the FNDI purpose or mission—a part of it, not separate from it.

The initial challenge was to provide a process that engaged the whole staff in brainstorming operating principles that fit each of the unique and varied positions at FNDI. The staff identified 144 operating principles or standards. After extensive negotiations, the 144 original standards were reduced to 33. At this point, the operating principles, their grouping under the evaluation framework, and the holistic interplay of functions that reflected a noncategorical, organic approach were in place. Exhibit 12.1 sets forth the 33 standards, with minor editing for parallel construction.

Working with supervisors, evaluation committee members met with employees to hammer out performance indicators that truly reflected both the job itself and the overarching mission and culture of the organization. This development

Control of Assets	Kinship
Effective and efficient control of FNDI's assets will ensure our sustainability into the future. Consistent control of assets will accommodate our collective abilities to recognize, manage, and comprehend our resources, ultimately facilitating our mission to assist Native people in developing community-controlled reservation economies. • Recognize opportunities. • Manage time effectively. • Give direct, timely feedback. • Set goals and deadlines. • Be attentive to details. • Manage the balance between information and action. • Produce high-quality work. • Know the limitations of resources. • Use resources appropriately. • Know how to share your expertise internally and externally.	Appreciating a strong internal kinship network is critical to the successful circulation and dissemination of First Nations assets as resources. The relationship between control of assets and kinship is dependent upon the staff's practice of sharing, appreciating, and respecting each other, as well as our constituents. • Respect individual differences. • Do not defend failure as success. • Share and celebrate successes. • Understand that your time frame may not coincide with others. • Make responses on values and decisions, rather than on moods and conditions. • Represent First Nations in a good light. • Understand the way individual departments fit First Nations as a whole. • Understand everyone's equal importance, while recognizing a decision-making process.

Exhibit 12.1. FNDI Table of Standards.

Personal Efficacy	Spirituality
Control of assets and kinship are necessary to take First Nations resources (people, money, materials) and share them throughout Indian Country. To accomplish this, First Nations colleagues must have confidence and pride in their work, and have an anticipatory, forward-thinking approach to their work. Strong personal efficacy within individuals will promote the overall success of First Nations.	The spirituality of First Nations allows us to make choices and decisions and prepare for our future. Inherent within it is our culture, and a common understanding that we are privileged to be involved with such important work. Also intermingled with our culture is the desire to strive for a balance.
<ul><li>Lead by example.</li><li>Take risks and accept responsibility for your actions.</li><li>Anticipate and follow up.</li><li>Learn from your mistakes.</li><li>Work toward self-enhancement.</li><li>Think of criticism as an opportunity for learning.</li><li>Take initiative to get the job done.</li><li>Know your job.</li><li>Think as an entrepreneur.</li></ul>	<ul><li>Be good humored.</li><li>Have a balance in your life.</li><li>Understand FNDI's culture and mission.</li><li>Understand the uniqueness of Native people and their culture.</li><li>Take advantage of the unique opportunities to change the lives of Indian people.</li><li>Be respectful of others.</li></ul>

of indicators to measure progress in itself was a learning process, as staff identified behaviors, standards, or specific goals for their positions—not themselves personally—against which they would be evaluated.

Once indicators had been identified and individuals oriented to the evaluative thinking behind the corporate standards, FNDI had an evaluation tool with culturally sensitive, practical footing and a powerful philosophy behind it. A few examples of performance indicators for field operations positions illustrate how the standards were interpreted within the evaluation framework:

- Control of Assets

  Run effective, efficient meetings.

  Be fiscally responsible.

Use travel budget carefully.

Prepare and monitor department budget.

Know when to cut losses.

- Kinship

Manage field staff to develop their capabilities.

Praise staff for results achieved and realized.

Address staff problems directly as soon after they occur as possible.

Understand the way in which individual departments fit into FNDI as a whole, and reinforce its mission.

Coordinate with other departments such as research to help them get their jobs in the field accomplished.

- Personal Efficacy

Manage time so you do not have to be managed.

Respond to technical assistance requests in a timely manner.

Take opportunities to serve on various committees in an effort to effect change.

- Spirituality
Understand the need to allow humor to reduce and eliminate stress.

A final word on spirituality. Within a Native worldview, spirituality affects everything. It is most difficult to describe and even harder to measure. However, spirituality connects with the other three quadrants (assets, kinship, and personal efficacy) in a way that produces outcomes consistent with the Native culture. All FNDI operating principles somehow reflect a spiritual dimension—a system of values and beliefs. It was intended that FNDI staff, in complying with the standards, would demonstrate gains that might well be considered as much values-based as technical skills–driven. This in fact occurred. Somewhere in the evaluation process, several staff members began volunteering for the first time at the local women's abuse center, literacy project, and free clinic. Several campaigns for Red Cross, local school computers, and the city homeless shelter were initiated as well. A renewed appreciation for serving people showed strongly among individual staff members and collectively among FNDI as a group of servant leaders.

Eagle Staff Fund Evaluation Description

The Eagle Staff Fund is a grant making and technical assistance project FNDI launched in 1993. It is the only national, Native American–controlled project that combines both grassroots community development grants and education to Native American communities with a policy approach to address the structural causes of Native American poverty. Grants are made to tribes, Native American organizations, or Native individuals who are launching or expanding community-based economic development initiatives.

It is the first of its kind, in whom it targets, the nature of its collaborative effort (between its foundation and corporate funders, grantees, and FNDI), its outreach and services to grant seekers, and its *noncategorical* approach to grant making. The Eagle Staff Fund's grassroots approach to community revitalization integrates social empowerment and spirituality with a community's economic needs, resulting in projects that address housing, the environment, health and nutrition, youth, leadership development, education, and technology. In April 1996, FNDI President Rebecca L. Adamson received the Council on Foundation's Robert W. Scrivner Award for creative and innovative grant making for the establishment of the Eagle Staff Fund.

The Eagle Staff Fund's four grant types correspond to a project's or organization's level of knowledge, capacity, and need: Seed Grants are under $5,000; Start-Up Grants are usually under $30,000; Working Capital Grants are between $30,000 and $100,000, made over a year or more; and Development Capital Grants are up to $150,000 annually, up to three years.

The significance of the Eagle Staff Fund evaluation is that it will validate in the mainstream society the holistic worldview of indigenous peoples—that all things are interconnected and that spirituality and culture are as essential to success as money—and probably even more so. The effect of this validation and dissemination of the evaluation results is that the philanthropic community (particularly categorical funders such as foundations and corporations) may recognize the value of a holistic approach, and may be more open to funding indigenous peoples on their own terms.

The evaluation will also serve as a vehicle for Native Americans to articulate their values and priorities to those outside their communities. Often, the worldview posed by the Elements of Development framework is known intuitively in Native communities, but people there may not have been able to express it on their own due to the difficulty of articulating cultural meanings.

In addition, the evaluation will provide feedback on Eagle Staff Fund operations, allowing FNDI to adapt or change systems while the project is in progress, institutionalizing its learning process for this project to serve Native Americans.

The Eagle Staff Fund evaluation is being conducted by an assessment team comprising consultants external to FNDI (Aspen Institute's Rural Communities Program and Cornerstone Consultants) in cooperation with FNDI staff to ensure its accuracy and objectivity. An advisory committee of Native people from various fields and Native and non-Native experts in evaluation and sustainable development oversees, advises, and assists in the evaluation. The Levi Strauss Foundation has funded FNDI participation in the evaluation; the Hitachi, Charles Stewart Mott, Ford, and Kellogg Foundations have funded the external team.

The evaluation team, advisory committee, and FNDI staff are undertaking the actual process of the evaluation: assembling and analyzing data; conducting interviews with grantees, potential and rejected grantees, funders, and others; conducting "co-learning" events for evaluation participants and grantee focus groups; and producing and disseminating interim and final reports. The methodology, developed by the consultants mentioned earlier and On Purpose Associates, will collect data from Eagle Staff Fund grant records, participating funders, and grantees, and through three multiyear case studies of communities in which grantees work. The data collection tools to be used include grant logs maintained by Eagle Staff Fund personnel; structured interviews with grantees, funders, and Eagle Staff Fund personnel; grantee focus groups; and case studies. For the case studies, the assessment team will work with grantees to develop and use impact measures and data collection instruments that reflect both the grantee's and the community's project objectives.

The assessment team and FNDI staff meet to go over these data. The group will look for patterns that will inform decisions about Eagle Staff Fund ongoing program improvements, and will also document the impact of Eagle Staff Fund grant making and technical assistance.

Working Hypotheses for the Eagle Staff Fund

The adoption of the Elements of Development framework for the Eagle Staff Fund evaluation is premised on the belief that development of a sustainable economy occurs when the relationships among assets, kinship, personal efficacy, and spirituality are understood and controlled by all the participants in a community. In the Eagle Staff Fund model, this development process moves about a balance among the quadrants of personal efficacy (human development), control of assets (economic development), spirituality (values), and kinship (community development). The circle graphically presents FNDI's theory of development as it plays out in sixteen elements among four quadrants. It also portrays the continuity and balance sought among the elements.

In the Eagle Staff Fund's work, this development is facilitated through a relationship between grantee and Eagle Staff Fund personnel—a relationship built on an understanding of the process of development as multidimensional and self-discovered, focusing on an understanding of the relationships among the elements.

In conducting the evaluation, FNDI seeks increasing clarity about the theory underlying its work. This theory will be modified and improved as this project progresses so that it more simply and accurately reflects the work that Eagle

Staff Fund is doing. The current statement of the theory emphasizes the importance that FNDI places on the relationships its staff builds with grantees and their understanding of the connections among the elements that they see at the heart of successful development.

Framework for Continuous Learning and Assessment

The four areas of focus of the evaluation will be Eagle Staff Fund operations (making grants, providing technical assistance, learning from the process), grantees (affecting their communities), Eagle Staff Fund funders (learning about Indian Country, bringing the two worlds closer), and the Elements of Development and their usefulness for planning, implementing, and monitoring development. When people understand that economic development is connected to everything else in their experience, FNDI believes, they contribute more powerfully to economic well-being, and they do so in more culturally appropriate ways. FNDI also hopes to improve its development hypothesis by learning from grantees' and practitioners' experiences.

These categories will cover the interests of each of several different audiences for the assessment's results. The primary audience is the board, management, and staff of FNDI. Other audiences include the Eagle Staff Fund funders, the broader philanthropic community, the grantees, economic development professionals—both in Indian Country and around the world—as well as nonprofit organizations and the media. While each audience is focused primarily on some subset of the information to be gained, when taken together, all this information will enable staff, the grant-making committees, the FNDI Board, and the Project Advisory Committee, funders, and current and potential grantees to learn about the impact—perceived and potential—of the Eagle Staff Fund.

The development of the methodology has been guided by several underlying principles:

- *Data collection tools are designed so that they can be included in the natural flow of work of Eagle Staff Fund and its projects.* The assessment team provides the framework for continuous learning and assessment and is responsible for refining and focusing the tools used. The tools and framework are designed so that the learning process can continue well beyond the time frame of the assessment project.

- *All stakeholders will actively participate in generating information and finding patterns within that information.* Therefore, the data will be collected by the assessment team, FNDI staff, and grantees. This collaboration increases the likelihood that the patterns discovered will result in behavior changes. In addition, the multiple perspectives contributing to the work will make the information richer.

- *Success will be measured by the grantees' self-defined indicators.* The assessment team will work with Eagle Staff Fund personnel, grantees, and three model communities to provide a consistent framework for the development and use of these indicators. Part of this framework entails the application of standards in selecting indicators to meet two criteria:

At least one of the indicators will address community impact as differentiated from process or output indicators.

In all grants over $5,000, at least one indicator will be economic.

The development and use of these indicators will be a part of the technical assistance that Eagle Staff Fund provides to all its grantees.

Plan for Data Gathering and Continuous Learning

The assessment design specifies how data will be gathered and organized, providing a foundation for exploration of the patterns that are revealed through this information to inform and improve the operations and theoretical foundation of Eagle Staff Fund.

Data Gathering. Six sources of data track the Eagle Staff Fund grant-making process:

A *project log*. Eagle Staff Fund staff keep a log during their work with each applicant during the process of inquiry, technical assistance, application or referral, project development, success indicator selection, recommendation, and approval or decline. They also log their observations as grantees implement projects, collect data, report results, learn, and plan next steps.

A series of *in-depth interviews*. After the grant is awarded and annually through the course of multiyear grants, the assessment team will conduct in-depth interviews with all Development Capital grantees, 50 percent of Working Capital grantees, and 30 percent of both Seed and Start-Up grantees.

A *postproject interview*. The assessment team will talk with the same groups of grantees after their projects conclude.

A set of *long-term case studies*. The assessment team, the FNDI president, the Eagle Staff Fund director, and the program officer will make an annual site visit to study three grantees and their community beneficiaries in each of the three years of assessment.

A series of *grantee focus groups*. Grantees representing varying regions and project sectors will meet once a year in focus group sessions conducted by the assessment team.

Eagle Staff Fund *funder interviews*. The assessment team will meet annually with funders to get their view of the process.

Continuous Learning. The assessment team will take the data collected from these six sources and present it to Eagle Staff Fund personnel and management three times each year so that patterns can be discerned and discussed. The team expected—and is finding—that the data will lead to new questions, and that some initial questions will yield information that is not particularly useful. So this stage of data collection and analysis will provide an opportunity to improve the data collection tools and influence how effectively they are being used.

As expected, the team is finding that this information can guide Eagle Staff Fund personnel in evaluating key process factors—from how they use their time to the content and presentation of the technical assistance they provide. Gradually, enough information will become available to enable Eagle Staff Fund personnel and other stakeholders to explore the relationships among the elements on the Development Wheel, as well as the strategic importance of each element itself. Finally, this information will guide the decisions that FNDI must make about the role of the funding collaborative after its three-year test.

Each year, the advisory committee will examine the results of the data collection and analysis conducted by Eagle Staff Fund and the assessment team. Advisory committee members will offer additional learning from their respective fields that relate to the Eagle Staff Fund findings. Committee insights will be very useful in exploring how the Wheel could be used to plan, implement, and monitor development, and to refine and improve the underlying development hypotheses.

Annually, the assessment team and FNDI will present to Eagle Staff Fund funders what they are learning about Eagle Staff Fund through data collection and analysis, the three Eagle Staff Fund assessment team–FNDI meetings per year, and the advisory committee meetings. Individually and collectively, the funders will also enrich the learning through their knowledge of Native American or community development projects both on and off reservations.

Taken together, all these stages of pattern seeking will help FNDI learn what is working and why. This knowledge will form the basis for ongoing improvements in Eagle Staff Fund operation. Moreover, this methodology embodies the premise underlying the personal efficacy element of FNDI's Development Wheel: people have their own answers within them, and when they obtain enough information and perspective to understand the patterns that are emerging, they can make powerful and appropriate changes.

SUMMARY

The approach to ongoing evaluation advocated in this volume is particularly suited to be sensitive to the unique cultural characteristics of organizations and groups within which programs and projects operate. The focus on learning and program and organizational effectiveness implicitly requires attention to the unique values, objectives, and underlying assumptions that influence behavior in organizations, groups, and programs.

The case study describes one organization's initiative to achieve organizational effectiveness in a culturally sensitive manner. The case further illustrates the breadth of cultural implications in a wide range of evaluation or assessment applications. The organization has found close parallels in its initiatives with internal annual staff assessments and with the evaluations it is conducting of its development grant project.

In recognition of the importance of culture in framing and carrying out organization and program evaluation, the evaluator will need to pay attention to the underlying assumptions, values, and motivations of the group or organization within which the program or project is being implemented. This suggests extreme caution with regard to imported views of the way things work and of imposed evaluation frameworks. As culture emerges from the basic underlying assumptions of a group, so evaluation design and methods should emerge from the values, beliefs, and objectives of the group within which the program operates. Although an outside observer may see the behavior of a group or the operation of a program as irrational, that behavior may be quite rational in the context of the group's own culture.

The new emphasis on this perspective should not compromise evaluation design, methods, or reliability. It will require more emphasis on process, case studies, and other qualitative methods. It is incremental improvement that is sought, which in the long run will more effectively lead to achievement of targeted outcomes. This approach assumes an understanding of the dynamic and ever-changing nature of human systems and the consequent rejection of approaches that assume a stable situation from which research and evaluation can prove or predict. This requires greater humility on the part of evaluation professionals and program managers. We can only be self-confident about learning, which is ongoing. Knowing, or certainty, in the behaviors and results in human systems is transient—replaced or refined by ongoing learning.

References

Fine, G. A., and Kleinman, S. "Rethinking Subculture: An Interactionist Analysis." *American Journal of Sociology,* 1979, *85*(1), 1–20.

Howard, G. S. "Culture Tales: A Narrative Approach to Thinking, Cross-Cultural Psychology, and Psychotherapy." *American Psychologist,* 1991, *46*(3), 187–197.

Hughes, D., Seidman, E., and Williams, N. "Cultural Phenomena and the Research Enterprise: Toward a Culturally Anchored Methodology." *American Journal of Community Psychology,* 1993, *21*(6), 687–703.

Kirkhart, K. E. "Multicultural Validity: A Postcard from the Road." *Evaluation Practice,* 1995, *16*(1), 1–12.

Klitgaard, R. "Including Culture in Evaluation Research." In R. Picciotto and R. C. Rist (eds.), *Evaluating Country Development Policies and Programs: New Approaches for a New Agenda.* New Directions for Evaluation, no. 67. San Francisco: Jossey-Bass, 1995.

Mair, M. "Psychology as Storytelling." *International Journal of Personal Construct Psychology,* 1988, *1,* 125–137.

Petrie, H. G. "Purpose, Context, and Synthesis: Can We Avoid Relativism?" In D. M. Fournier (ed.), *Reasoning in Evaluation: Inferential Leaps and Links.* New Directions for Evaluation, no. 68. San Francisco: Jossey-Bass, 1995.

Putnam, R. S., with Leonardi, R., and Nanetti, R. Y. *Making Democracy Work: Civic Traditions in Modern Italy.* Princeton, N.J.: Princeton University Press, 1993.

Schein, E. H. *Organizational Culture and Leadership.* (2nd ed.) San Francisco: Jossey-Bass, 1992.

CHAPTER THIRTEEN

Using Outside Evaluators

Patricia Patrizi
James R. Sanders

The evaluation philosophy underlying this book is populist, participatory, pragmatic. It recognizes that all participants in a program, an organization, or a community are, in many respects, evaluators, even though they may not call their decision-making processes *evaluation*. They all have experiences, training, and perspectives that they regularly employ in an everyday manner as they assess their own work and that of others around them.

In this chapter we offer a perspective on evaluation designed to maximize this resource and potential. No one is all-knowing and no one evaluator can have all the pertinent information available when making every judgment. No one can even represent all the values held by the multiple participants or affected parties. Consequently, in this view of evaluation we try to empower as many people as we can—the receptionist, the client, the service provider, the bookkeeper, the CEO, the board, the volunteers, funders, and others—to see themselves as the evaluators. Everyone can ask good questions, can be observant, can share information and lessons gained from experience, and can identify areas for change based on experience. The assumption we make is that only this kind of involvement of stakeholders will enable a program, organization, or community to continuously improve. This is how we get better at what we do. It all seems so rational.

Yet we rarely activate the full array of evaluation resources at our disposal. Agencies and community groups have historically sought the assessment of others outside the organization as the only credible source of judgment. The theory behind this view is that only those external to an organization can arrive at an objective assessment and, conversely, that the judgments of those inside an organization are necessarily tainted by their proximity to the work under review. While there is some truth to these ideas, it is equally true that it is often extremely difficult for external evaluators to arrive at a full understanding of the work at hand. Given the complexity of societal problems and organizational life, external evaluators are always and necessarily working with incomplete knowledge.

The field of evaluation has belatedly become aware of this conundrum and has responded with a range of approaches—participatory evaluation, self-evaluation, empowerment evaluation, and action research—all directed toward self-inquiry and reflection. We call participants in a program, organization, or community who assess its performance *participant-evaluators*.

Facilitating a process of self-reflection, however, is a delicate business. It is important for us to consider qualities of a good evaluator, including training, interpersonal skills, group facilitation skills, and ultimately wisdom—as well as how these characteristics lend themselves to an appropriate role in a participatory evaluation. It is extraordinarily easy for participant-evaluators, in light of traditional approaches to evaluation and technical concerns, to turn the reins over to so-called professionals. Likewise, many professional evaluators far too easily assume the role of expert, thereby undermining the authority of the participants. In both cases, genuine self-reflection and judgment are quashed.

This is not to say that participant-evaluators must be formally trained in evaluation. On the contrary, we would argue that participant-evaluators should take the lead in inviting in outside help when they need it. The important point is that they should recognize when they need an outside consultant, and then they should seek a qualified evaluation specialist who has the skills and insight they require.

So what then becomes a useful and effective role for the outside professional evaluator in this light? This chapter discusses ways outside expertise can enhance the participant-evaluation process. It concludes with advice about how to select a qualified outside evaluation specialist.

ROLES FOR AN OUTSIDE EVALUATION CONSULTANT

We see five ways in which a good outside evaluator can improve the quality of evaluation being done by an organization:

- Helping to ask good questions
- Designing systematic ways to gather information
- Drawing defensible conclusions

- Facilitating a reflective process
- Reviewing and improving the whole system of evaluation

Helping to Ask Good Questions

Good outside evaluators ask good questions, supplementing those of the participant-evaluators. The outside evaluator should push the operating assumptions that may inadvertently constrain or distort the questions of participants. By good questions, we mean questions that systematically address the range of issues that need to be addressed. Good evaluation specialists can also discriminate between trivial and important questions, by using such criteria as:

- Who would be upset if this question is dropped?
- Is the answer self-evident or already available?
- Would the answer reduce current uncertainty among participants?
- Would we miss an important aspect of the program, organization, or community if the question were dropped?
- Can we answer the question?
- Are there alternate theories that better explain the outcome of an intervention or the nature of a particular problem?

Probably the simplest model to stimulate participant questioning and reflection is *systems thinking*. Systems models should generate, when well used, thinking about inputs, processes, and outcomes (and their interrelationships). Systems thinking serves as a framework for contexts and influential actors in a field or environment, thereby generating the kind of thoughtful deliberation that produces high-quality solutions and improvements in the way a system functions.

Another well-known model—the *CIPP model*—leads one to ask questions about *context* (needs of clients, existing resources), *inputs* (the competing strategies for addressing needs that should be considered when planning), *processes* (how the plan is working, identifying where changes are needed), and *products* (interim, short-term or immediate, and long-term changes that are taking place). This process should identify and clarify important evaluative questions. These questions then become the focal point for subsequent observations and discussion.

When employing either of these models, the role an external evaluation consultant can play is that of facilitator or coach. In this role the external evaluator elicits questions and prods participant-evaluators to think in areas that may not initially be considered. Many insights can come from having a qualified outsider ask questions or getting participants to ask questions that they might not have thought of otherwise.

Designing Systematic Ways to Gather Information

Participant-evaluators are typically not trained in technical skill areas such as instrument development, sampling, and research design. A good consultant with a strong background in the social sciences can be called in as needed to assist with the design of a questionnaire, to select a sample for a survey, or to train interviewers. Consultants may be called in to help select appropriate measures or indicators of performance or to set up a management information system. These are technical skills that one can buy as needed. The participant-evaluators know what they want to learn (perhaps with help of an outside consultant), they communicate it or their priorities to the evaluation consultant, and they review the consultant's work to make sure that they are getting what they want. This is a very different scenario from delegating the full evaluation to an external evaluator, because now the participant-evaluators are in control of the evaluation process.

Drawing Defensible Conclusions

One of the most difficult challenges for any evaluator is to be able to reach a conclusion that is defensible but bold enough to inspire action. External evaluators can at times hide behind an empirical facade, hampering conclusions under the weight of qualifying statements—on one hand, it looks like this is happening . . . on the other hand, you may prefer . . . but also. . . . Alternately, participant-evaluators not trained in the social sciences can be led astray by information they collect for evaluation purposes. Overheard conversations, person-on-the-street interviews, opinions voiced in a focus group, and comments taken out of context can all be misleading if interpreted in the wrong way. In addition, participant-evaluators may need help in remaining impartial as they evaluate their own efforts. We all have operating theories regarding the nature of a problem and the viability and appropriateness of certain solutions. It is human to allow our biases to lead us to both evidence and conclusions that confirm our initial assumptions. It takes detachment and fortitude to explore the strength of our fundamental assumptions, although it is that kind of exploration that produces authentic learning. An outside consultant trained in the social sciences can advise a participant-evaluator group on where the pitfalls of logic are and how to avoid them.

Participant-evaluators may also call an evaluation specialist to help with compiling and interpreting the information that is available to them. Experienced evaluation specialists are good for bringing order from seemingly chaotic conditions and cutting through information overload. Specialists have been trained in methods for creating categories of evidence and in looking for patterns and trends that may be invisible to the untrained eye. They also have computer software that can help bring order, especially from qualitative information.

Finally, we must always be concerned with putting findings into context when drawing conclusions. A trained outside eye can help participant-evaluators look at findings in light of the environment in which the program, organization, or community has been operating. Political, social, economic, technical, and human factors can all lead to important qualifications of conclusions.

For example, when judging the progress of a homeless shelter in reducing the level of substance abuse among the people it serves, it will be important to take into consideration the difficulty of bringing about change. Sometimes small changes in the right direction, although they may be costly and take a great amount of time, may be worth the effort in terms of longer-term returns. Alternately, there are certain indicators of progress that are relatively useless with certain subpopulations. Because of an artifact of measurement or some feature of the population under study, the outcomes of interest simply may never be affected. Moreover, some findings may be affected by untoward changes in the environment such as those emanating from regulatory, fiscal, or social and demographic shifts. Participant-evaluators, without an understanding of either the technical or sociopolitical context of such change, may need outside advice when drawing conclusions.

One of the techniques of the evaluation specialist is the use of a heterogeneous focus group called an *interpretation panel* to review information and to allow the members of the group to interpret it from their own perspective. The focus group members are given the information and time to write down their own thoughts about it, that is, to say what it means to them. Then they read their interpretations aloud before group discussion begins. The outside evaluation specialist serves as facilitator and also as one of the interpreters so that yet another perspective is added into the mix.

Within this framework, the role of the outside evaluator when conclusions are being drawn is one of observing the process and reviewing the conclusions to make sure there are no logical flaws. Evaluators trained in the social sciences should be well equipped to play this role. Although some separate reflection on the part of the outside evaluator may be necessary, it is certainly not the role of the external evaluation consultant to draw conclusions in the complete absence of participants, given the philosophy behind ongoing evaluation.

Facilitating a Reflective Process

One of the most useful roles played by an external evaluation consultant is that of facilitator to a process of self-evaluation. The more disparate views that can be brought to the table, the richer the discussion—in theory. In reality, organizational life is fraught with relatively entrenched positions. Similarly, communities have well-established patterns of interaction and problem resolution that can benefit from the mediation and analytic capacities of an external evaluator. A skillful consultant can assist in bringing differing positions to light, and can facilitate a probing analysis of the relative merits of alternative and potentially conflicting paths. The role of the consultant is that of coinvestigator and facilitator, but not that of judge.

Reviewing and Improving the Whole System of Evaluation

Evaluation specialists are trained to use *meta-evaluation*—evaluation of evaluation processes—as part of any evaluation system. They realize that any evaluation process itself can be flawed and that it is important to detect and then correct those flaws before any damage is done.

The Program Evaluation Standards (Joint Committee on Standards for Educational Evaluation, 1994) was produced to assist evaluators in reviewing their work, and evaluation specialists should be aware of and use these standards. An outside evaluation specialist could be asked to apply the standards to the way in which an organization was doing evaluation. The results would provide a useful guide to improving the evaluation process. In essence, a review like this every two years could help an organization make sure that its ongoing evaluation process was useful, feasible, proper, and accurate. It could also give the group guidance for taking it the next step in its development.

HOW TO SELECT A QUALIFIED OUTSIDE EVALUATOR

In the absence of any kind of certification or licensing systems for evaluation specialists, those who would like to bring in an outside evaluator are often left to word-of-mouth recommendations or their own judgment. Word of mouth is a good system if others have had good experiences with an accessible evaluation specialist's work on the same tasks that are of current interest. However, a local organization often finds it difficult or impossible to get recommendations for a consultant who has already been successful with the specific assignment in question. In these frequent cases evaluation specialists may be asked to submit their qualifications for the participant-evaluators to review.

One evaluation text (Worthen and Sanders, 1987, pp. 178–180) lists five ways for judging evaluator qualifications:

- *Formal academic preparation.* Graduates of specialized evaluation programs are few and far between. Such programs, however, do focus attention on the full array of processes described in this chapter. For the most part you should look to educational experience in the social sciences, which place value on the conceptual and analytic capacities we have discussed. For instance, within this framework you should look for the ability to think systemically, offer alternative and provocative theories regarding problems and their solutions, use the range of data collection and analysis skills best suited to respond to your information needs, and apply evaluation standards.

- *Evaluation experience.* Look here for experience in a range of technical approaches to evaluation. For instance, evaluators who have worked exclusively in the case study approach will tend to prefer that method, regardless of whether it is the most suitable one for your needs. The evaluator should demonstrate at least a working familiarity with both qualitative and quantitative methods, although he or she will understandably have preferences. In addition, you should examine the consultant's background in terms of project management experience to determine whether it demonstrates the skills necessary to address the complexity of your information needs.

- *Evaluation philosophy or orientation.* The well-established traditions within evaluation tend to work against the more egalitarian philosophy underlying participant evaluation approaches. It is important to examine the consultant's capacity to work collegially and out of the traditional box of hierarchical evaluation. References and experience should speak to this point.

- *Track record, recommendations.* Practice does make perfect in this arena. Weak evaluators rarely get repeat work. A broad number and range of clients are other indicators of survival in a competitive field. Feel free to ask for multiple recommendations and to call these clients yourself.

- *Personal style and characteristics.* Although listed last, this should be first among your priorities. The other capacities are necessary, but they can be spread among several consultants. Personal style and, more important, genuine wisdom are the sine qua non of excellence in evaluation. While these characteristics may be somewhat difficult to find, they are well worth the search.

To these we would add a question about whether the evaluation consultant belongs to a professional evaluation association such as the American Evaluation Association (AEA), and also a question about use of the *Program Evaluation Standards.* We would also ask for a reaction to the work of INDEPENDENT SECTOR on the approach to ongoing evaluation described in this book.

SUMMARY

We certainly support the integration of evaluation into the routines of organizations in the nonprofit sector. We see evaluation as the lifeblood of organizations that are changing and will continue to be undergoing change.

From time to time outside evaluators can play a role in helping the organization refine its practices. We have described five roles in this chapter. We have also added our thoughts about how to select an outside evaluator when this action is seen as necessary or helpful. Everything we have said has come from the viewpoint that all people are evaluators—participant-evaluators—and that evaluation specialists are ideally used to enhance ongoing evaluation practices that should occur in any organization seeking continuous improvement.

References

Joint Committee on Standards for Educational Evaluation. *The Program Evaluation Standards.* Thousand Oaks, Calif.: Sage, 1994.

Worthen, B. R., and Sanders, J. R. *Educational Evaluation.* Reading, Mass.: Addison Wesley Longman, 1987.

How the New Approach Was Developed

Sandra Trice Gray

Evaluation is an ongoing process to achieve organizational effectiveness, empowerment of people, and ultimately excellence in the achievement of mission, involving all stakeholders and including all aspects of the organization. It ideally creates an environment for organizational learning and renewal.

INDEPENDENT SECTOR, in its continuous effort to promote and help organizations maintain their effectiveness, engaged in a process to focus the sector's attention on evaluation as a means to increased effectiveness. Increasing pressure on nonprofit organizations—to compete for funding, justify tax dollars, satisfy constituencies, confirm the public trust, and ensure survival—makes it imperative that institutions become more adept at assessing their own effectiveness, integrating a process of ongoing evaluation into the total organization, and using the information for improvement and renewal.

The overall outcome of the process was to enhance the attitudes and behavior of the sector with respect to evaluation as a means to increased effectiveness and fulfillment of mission.

The process had three focus areas:

- Increasing interest and commitment to evaluation and renewal
- Making resources available to the sector
- Helping organizations use evaluation results for learning, renewal, and institutional survival

To address the first focus area, INDEPENDENT SECTOR sponsored Regional Roundtables in six locations around the country. The purpose of the Regional Roundtables was twofold: INDEPENDENT SECTOR would discover what organizations want, need, and will use to assist them in their own evaluation in order to assemble or develop resources to meet those needs, and participants would develop greater commitment to evaluation to see the need and the benefit to their own organization and increase their interest in ongoing organizational and program effectiveness.

OVERVIEW OF REGIONAL AND NATIONAL ROUNDTABLES

A pilot Regional Roundtable was conducted in Kansas City. Regional Roundtables were held in Seattle, San Francisco, New York, Atlanta, and Chicago. National Roundtables were convened in Minneapolis, San Francisco, and Washington, D.C. Teams consisting of CEOs and board chairs from a cross-section of the sector's nonprofit organizations and representatives of foundations and corporate giving offices, academic centers, and the evaluation community were invited to attend each Roundtable.

The Roundtable Process

Roundtables were designed to be highly interactive and to stimulate dialogue within each team, as well as among participants from other organizations. It was intended that participants gain new insights and a fresh perspective on evaluation by exploring the subject with their peers. Participants were encouraged to put evaluation into the context of change and the future environment in which they will all operate.

There was an attempt to demystify evaluation and to define it as any activity designed to find out whether a given effort has or has not produced the intended results. Evaluation was described as the gathering of any kind of information an organization learns from, integrates into overall operations, and uses for ongoing improvement.

Central to the exploration of evaluation was the concept of *paradigms* and *paradigm shifts*. Participants identified paradigms (tacit understandings and rules that prevent the acceptance of new or conflicting information) that they currently associated with evaluation and discussed the ways in which those paradigms either supported or hindered effective evaluation. They also identified which paradigms needed to shift or change and what impact that might have on how people approached and implemented evaluation.

Finally, Roundtable participants were asked to contribute to a list of evaluation resources that they needed, wanted, and would use to better evaluate their own effectiveness. That discussion also generated a number of characteristics of those resources.

Prevailing Themes from the Roundtable Discussions

- *The relationship between grant makers and grant seekers plays an important role in evaluation.*

Nonprofit organizations reported that most of their evaluation efforts are done to fulfill the requirements of funding sources. They often feel overwhelmed with requirements and multiple evaluation formats. They believe funders do not place consistent importance on evaluation. Participants said that the models funders require often do not provide information the organization considers useful and relevant.

There were opportunities at several Roundtables for funder and nonprofit participants to share their perceptions of each other with respect to evaluation. Nonprofit organizations believe they cannot take "bad news" to funders for fear of risking future funding. They suspect that funders do not always take evaluation information into consideration in their funding and policy decisions. There is a perception that the most important evaluation criteria for funders are volume and numbers served.

At the same time, funders believe nonprofit organizations often resent their requests for evaluation and view them as punitive. Funders believe evaluation requests are perceived as costly, time consuming, and disruptive to the organization's program activities.

Both grant maker and grant seeker participants believed that greater collaboration and communication on decisions about criteria for effectiveness, as well as methods and processes, could serve as a relationship-building tool and create consensus among all stakeholders.

- *There is a need and a desire to make evaluation an ongoing and integrated part of an organization's life.*

Participants expressed a strong desire to move away from the prevailing opinion that evaluation is an annual event required by funders and "as soon as it is over, we can put it on the shelf and get back to our real work." Organizations want evaluation information to be used in planning and decision making and to be an efficient and ongoing part of doing business. Concerns center on staff and the time constraints and the extent to which ongoing evaluation activities would add to an already overburdened staff. There were requests for guidance, models, and methods to assist the organization in incorporating evaluation data into everyday operations.

- *There is a perceived void in information and methodology for evaluating outcomes.*

Most nonprofit organizations are stymied about how to approach evaluating the results of their efforts. Consequently, they rely almost entirely on volume measures, participant satisfaction data, compliance with standards, and information on participant characteristics.

Several persistent perceptions limit efforts to evaluate results. People regard cause-and-effect relationships as too difficult to track and measure over time, behavior change as too complex to assess, and costs as prohibitive. Even where these objections seem surmountable, prevention and advocacy activities present unique challenges to evaluation, and relatively few tools and resources are available for internal use.

- *Changing attitudes and beliefs about evaluation and the information it provides are a key factor in changing behavior.*

Participants believe that a change in attitudes and beliefs would make a great difference in how nonprofit organizations approach and implement evaluation. As participants discussed their current "paradigms" about evaluation, they concluded that many are limiting and unquestionably have an effect on how they approach and implement evaluation.

Here are some examples of paradigms that create obstacles to effective evaluation:

It takes time away from the "real work."

It requires experts and is expensive to do.

It has to be complex; simple isn't OK.

It is an event, with no impact on what we do.

It is too complicated and tedious.

It focuses only on what can be quantified.

If our work was successful in the past, it should continue to be successful.

If you can't prove success, resources will be taken away.

It must be quantitative, not qualitative.

We get no feedback and no reward from assessment.

You can't assess what we do.

You might have to change based on the results.

Intuitive judgment is often better than quantitative information.

Never assess the work of volunteers or board members (or you might lose them).

Assessment usually gives bad news.

If you are doing good work, you don't need to determine if you are working good.

You are more apt to get funding because of past successes or who you know than from good assessment results.

The assessment needs to make the foundation look good.

Quantity is what is important; it is more important than quality.

Here are the new mind-sets or new paradigms that Roundtable participants believed would enhance evaluation activities:

It is OK to fail and learn from it.

We evaluate our work to improve our own effectiveness, not just to satisfy our funders.

Assessment is not an add-on but important in its own right.

Assessment is a benefit, not a burden.

Incremental results are still results; success can come in incremental steps.

Assessment information is feedback, not failure.

Ongoing assessment will make us even more effective.

We must get beyond the human fear of being judged.

You can get useful information in short time frames from uncomplicated methods.

Our organization's mission will be strengthened through good assessment.

Grant makers and grant seekers can talk with each other, tell each other the truth and work together toward more effective assessment.

Interaction with the funder is a relationship, not a transaction.

Assessment does not have to be costly.

Assessment doesn't have to be done by the old rules; we can find creative new methods.

The time spent at assessment is well spent.

Assessment is a priority, not an option.

The goal of assessment is learning and improving.

Assessment can be an ongoing part of everyday work.

Everyone (funders, nonprofits, and clients) benefits from good assessment information.

We need assessment information so we can learn and change.

Changing what we do in the future does not diminish the value of what we have done in the past.

SUMMARY OF
NATIONAL ROUNDTABLES

The reflections and cautions that emerged from the discussions clustered around five issues surrounding our effort to reframe evaluation in search of institutional effectiveness in the sector. How do we sharpen the distinctions between the old and new paradigms of evaluation? What are the attributes of the new paradigm? How does this evaluation process help demonstrate accountability? It needs to be made clear that evaluation, under the new paradigm, is not an event but a process; not episodic, but ongoing; not outside the organization, but ingrained in its ongoing operations; not closed but open to all—inside and outside.

Agreement on the importance of centrality of mission and the pursuit of effectiveness as the impetus for evaluation. Consensus materialized on four points.

The Concept of Evaluation

Integral to evaluation are mission, planning, funding, marketing, and above all learning. Its attributes are flexibility in response to variable circumstances, adaptability to diverse cultures, collaboration, and ownership. Evaluation, as an analogue to accountability, needs a theory framed in the context of the distinctiveness of the nonprofit sector. It needs criteria to sort out what is appropriate versus inappropriate to mission, what is good versus bad performance, and what is effective versus ineffective in the pursuit of mission. The new vision is powerful and calls for a simple, compelling message, perhaps even a slogan.

Obstacles and Requirements

Five impediments in the sector affect evaluation. The obstacles include pervasive fear; lack of models; communication—the message, the medium, the receiver, and the language; absence of rewards and incentives; and cultural resistance.

There are needs for case studies, dissemination vehicles, networks, learning systems, pilot tests, awards, and champions. INDEPENDENT SECTOR has helped incubate this ongoing process of evaluation. It has deployed its resources as a convener, as a research center, and as a clearinghouse. But it is merely a parent in the process of developing the new process of evaluation. For its growth and maturation, *everyone in the sector must take ownership*.

The shift to a new paradigm. Participants turned to INDEPENDENT SECTOR to provide its constructive role as a catalyst for change in addressing this new paradigm on this evaluation agenda and to share the experiences continuously throughout the sector as to what works and what does not and why.

WHAT ROUNDTABLE PARTICIPANTS WANT, NEED, AND WILL USE

What participants most often requested was a means of sharing the evaluation experiences of other organizations, preferably organizations as similar to theirs as possible. They would like to know what worked and didn't work, what the organization learned or would do differently the next round of effectiveness assessment, how evaluation information was used in planning and decision making, and what happened as a result. In addition to sharing experiences, they want to share tools and methods that have proved valuable in other organizations. Participants want methods and skills to make evaluation an ongoing and integrated part of their everyday activities instead of an "event" that takes place primarily when required by a funder.

Organizations would use an evaluation guide or process—one that would help prepare everyone in the organization for either self-evaluation or evaluation provided by an outside source. This would include such things as who should be involved, decisions that need to be made, how to establish effectiveness criteria, and how to involve staff in the process.

Executive directors want staff to perceive evaluation as an opportunity to learn and improve and not as a threat to their job or a judgment about their value to the organization. Others asked for a do-it-yourself guide, broken into components, that could be tailored to meet the organization's special needs. It appears that most nonprofit organizations prefer to bring evaluation skills in-house and not rely on outside experts.

A central clearinghouse or information source was frequently mentioned, but one that is structured in a new way—easy to access and easy to use. A computer-based information source was often proposed.

Participants asked for better and easier methods and tools for measuring outcomes and results, especially those hard-to-measure activities such as behavior change, prevention, and advocacy.

Participants requested training evaluation methodology, wanted information on mentoring and peer review possibilities, and suggested that various outside resources be made available to assist an organization with its own evaluation.

Participants hope that INDEPENDENT SECTOR will continue to be a meeting ground to motivate, inspire, and help change organizational mind-sets so as to "move evaluation up on the list of priorities." They also see IS taking a role in bringing grant makers and grant seekers together to look at mutual solutions to evaluation issues.

USEFUL EVALUATION RESOURCES

Roundtable participants asked for "simple, low-cost, fast, and effective" evaluation methods and tools. They want new and different ways to assess their effectiveness as well as methods that are natural, free of jargon, less structured, and less formal. They would like evaluation resources that can be adapted to their own needs and idiosyncrasies. Participants frequently mentioned the desirability of using technology such as electronic bulletin boards for easily accessible information from a central source or computer-directed evaluation methodologies. They would like a menu of comprehensive tools covering all evaluation indices. Shared tools and methods that work in organizations similar to theirs are considered useful.

HOLISTIC APPROACH TO EVALUATION

Recurrent themes from discussion about the probable environment for nonprofit organizations in the foreseeable future were that there will be fewer resources available to meet greater needs. There will be increasing scrutiny and greater demand for nonprofit organizations to be effective and accountable. Although there will be more need for collaboration, networking, and cooperation in order to survive, the sector will be increasingly diverse, competitive, and divisive. Less reliance on the government will place increased pressure on the sector. Funders, clients, and the general public will be more demanding. The makeup of boards, volunteer groups, and staffs will be different.

Set in the context of the probable environment for nonprofit organizations, participants agreed that accurate and timely evaluation information will be an essential ingredient for future renewal and survival. The more rapidly the environment changes, the more critical evaluation information will be.

It was suggested that evaluation information allows the organization to focus its strategy, giving it the ability to say no to competing claims on limited resources. Participants noted that good evaluation information helps identify strengths and weaknesses, tests whether current objectives are reasonable and attainable, and helps the organization set reasonable goals for the future.

Roundtable information suggests that this project take a holistic approach to evaluation, one that takes into account several factors:

- *External environment.* Participants are broadening their horizons when they think about their resource base. They are looking beyond institutional funders and considering a variety of community resources, including local funders. The ideal relationship between a nonprofit organization and its funding sources with respect to evaluating results is one of collaboration and open communication. Participants see great benefit to the organization in collaboration and open communication. Participants see great benefit in forming partnerships with the grant maker to make sure that evaluation meets both parties' information needs. A partnership or collaborative effort between grant maker and grant seeker would do much to break down the paradigm that evaluation is something we do for *them,* not something we do for *us.*

- *Internal effectiveness.* Nonprofit organizations are more likely to attempt to measure the quantity or quality of their programs and services than they are to assess how effectively they manage their internal operations. Participants acknowledged the importance of assessing the effectiveness of their staff and how it manages the organization.

Roundtable participants report that internal effectiveness evaluation is often perceived as threatening and uncomfortable. Information that says change is needed suggests that what people have been working so hard at has not been adequate. A "failure-free learning environment" is ideal, but hard to achieve. Leadership within the organization that supports and encourages that kind of environment was cited as essential. It was also noted that some kind of bonus or nonmonetary reward system would do much to help staff embrace the idea of ongoing evaluation.

- *External results.* Although outcome-based evaluation is believed to be important, it is uncharted territory for most nonprofits. While it is generally acknowledged that a true measure of the impact of one's work is ideal, it is clear that, until they believe it is possible to measure results, participants want to have a variety of evaluation techniques available to them. They will continue to rely on measures such as volume, participant satisfaction, compliance with standards, and participant characteristics. At the same time, they hope in the future to find better ways to assess the results of their efforts.

- *Integration of evaluation into the organization's ongoing activities.* There is a need to help organizations get away from evaluation as an event and to institutionalize evaluation into the fabric of the organization. Organizations need better ways to think about and learn from evaluation information and to integrate it into their ongoing activities.

- *Language.* The sector needs to be speaking the same language with respect to this subject. Words related to effectiveness, evaluation, assessment, and results have different meanings among grant makers and grant seekers as well as in different subsectors, in different geographical areas, and among those who teach and write about the sector.

It was difficult at Roundtables to get people accustomed to the word *assessment*. *Evaluation* is more commonly used, although participants acknowledged that the term carries negative baggage, such as judgment, interruption, and a one-time event. At the time participants felt that a case could be made for using *assessment* consistently as a way to develop a *new* shared meaning for the word. This volume offers a new entrant to the contest for the language: *coevaluation*, but only time will tell whether it will take hold. An outcome for this project, no matter what term is used, is *shared meaning* among all parties.

CONCLUSION

Evaluation of some kind is reportedly occurring in almost all of the organizations that participated in the Regional Roundtables. Some have formal activities managed by part-time or, in a very few cases, full-time staff. Most use less formal methods and report that evaluation is not consistent; it does not cover *all* program activities *all* the time. Intuitive judgments are, in many cases, considered to be evaluation because they form the basis of decision making and planning.

Participants acknowledge, however, that what they are doing with respect to evaluation is not always valued, nor is it integrated into the day-to-day operations of the organization. There was keen interest in what other organizations are currently doing and an openness to hearing about existing methods, as well as learning new and different ways to evaluate effectiveness and impact.

The paradigm concept proved useful in helping participants get beyond the desire for methodology and confront their own mind-sets and beliefs about evaluation and the information it provides. Unless that information is deemed relevant and of value, no matter how accurately or creatively it is obtained, it will not be used for improvement or change.

To "enhance the attitudes and behavior of the sector with respect to evaluation," this project tackled the subject on many levels. First there had to be a change in how people think about evaluation. The sector needs a new paradigm, a new way of looking at evaluation. As is true in most change efforts, the challenge for this project will be greatest in the area of changing prevailing attitudes and beliefs.

INDEPENDENT SECTOR is pioneering a new paradigm for evaluation—a shift from old, inhibiting beliefs to new and enabling ones. It is seeking an evaluation process that addresses all independent sector organizations and suggests, among other elements, that ongoing evaluation:

- Is a process of asking good questions, gathering information to answer them, and making decisions based on those answers.

- Is a means of organizational learning—a way for the organization to assess its progress and change in ways that lead to greater achievement of its mission.

- Is an essential component of effective decision making, whether it be strategic planning or the decision making of daily organizational life. When evaluation is part of an organization's ongoing life, learning is valued because it provides the information necessary for continuous improvement.

- Is the responsibility of everyone. Everyone in the organization gathers information and asks What can we do to get better?

- Addresses the total system including internal effectiveness and external results.

- Is not an event, but a process; not episodic, but ongoing; not outside the organization, but ingrained in the day-to-day operations of the organization.

- Is a developmental process, not a report-card process.

- Occurs in an environment that is as risk free as possible, where people can examine why something succeeded or failed without fear of negative consequences.

- Is promoted by an organization's leadership, who already nurture a climate of trust and who value feedback as a way to assess progress and enhance effectiveness.

- Invites collaboration within an organization and with external parties such as clients, donors, and grantees.

- Employs tools and methodology that are accessible to organizations of all kinds and sizes. These simple, cost-effective, user-friendly evaluation methods can be adapted to meet each organization's needs and idiosyncracies.

- Is time and effort well spent, saves money in the long run by making better use of limited resources, and helps ensure the organization's health and viability in a changing environment.

BOARD MEETING EVALUATION FORM

Sandra Trice Gray

BOARD MEETING EVALUATION

(Please take a moment to evaluate this meeting.)

In the spirit of ongoing evaluation, did our collective work as a Board:

Using a scale of 5 (high) to 1 (low), circle your response

1. Keep the vision and mission central in all of our decision making?	5	4	3	2	1
2. Result in making only essential policy decisions?	5	4	3	2	1
3. Benefit from the agenda materials provided in advance of the meeting?	5	4	3	2	1
4. Benefit from the interactive processes used during the meeting (such as small group work, facilitated discussion of total board, framing of key questions for board reflection)?	5	4	3	2	1

General comment:_____

_____

_____

5. Help you to commit between
now and the next meeting to
work (with others) to achieve
the following?   5   4   3   2   1

(Please list)_____

_____

_____

_____

6. Reveal the questions we should consistently ask ourselves?
(Write questions)_____

_____

_____

_____

7. Reveal areas that our work as a board can be strengthened? (Please provide
feedback to the executive director and/or executive committee.)

_____

_____

_____

_____

8. Help you recommend the following one-year, two-year, five-year, and ongoing benchmarks to evaluate the Board's performance?
(Please list)_____

_____

_____

_____

BOARD OF DIRECTORS GOVERNANCE EVALUATION FORM

American Society of Association Executives

GOVERNANCE EVALUATION

Director Self-Evaluation

Circle your response using this scale:

5   =   Very satisfied
1   =   Not at all satisfied
NS =   Not sure

I. FOCUS ON STRATEGIC DIRECTION

How satisfied are you
that you

A. Understand the organization's vision, mission, and strategic goals?	5	4	3	2	1	NS
B. Kept the vision and strategic plan in mind during board discussions?	5	4	3	2	1	NS
C. Communicated *your* ideas for the organization's future direction?	5	4	3	2	1	NS

D. Minimized discussion on the organization's operations and maximized discussion on vision and strategic direction?	5	4	3	2	1	NS

II. BOARD FUNCTION

How satisfied are you that you

A. Have read the bylaws recently?	5	4	3	2	1	NS
B. Are knowledgeable about major programs and services?	5	4	3	2	1	NS
C. Understand the organization's financial statements?	5	4	3	2	1	NS
D. Make knowledgeable and prudent decisions about finances?	5	4	3	2	1	NS
E. Effectively represent the organization members, allied societies, the public, and others?	5	4	3	2	1	NS

III. BOARD EFFECTIVENESS

How satisfied are you that you

A. Understand your responsibilities as director as described in the role and responsibilities statement?	5	4	3	2	1	NS
B. Execute your responsibilities?	5	4	3	2	1	NS
C. Are familiar with the board's committee structure?	5	4	3	2	1	NS
D. Prepare for board meetings by reading agenda materials?	5	4	3	2	1	NS
E. Actively participate in board discussions?	5	4	3	2	1	NS

F. Represent the
membership's interests and
concerns during board
discussions?   5   4   3   2   1   NS

G. Accept work assignments?   5   4   3   2   1   NS

IV. GENERAL

A. Please rate your overall
performance as a director.   5   4   3   2   1   NS

B. Please indicate how
satisfying and rewarding you
find your board service to be. 5   4   3   2   1   NS

C. What can be done to
make your board service
more satisfying?

_____

_____

_____

_____

_____

BOARD OF DIRECTORS
GOVERNANCE APPRAISAL FORM

American Society of Association Executives

BOARD OF DIRECTORS GOVERNANCE APPRAISAL

Circle your response using this scale:

5 = Strongly agree

1 = Strongly disagree

I. BOARD FUNCTION

Evaluate how well the board of directors carries out its major responsibilities: advancing the vision, promoting the mission, engaging in strategic planning, fulfilling its fiduciary responsibility, monitoring programs and services, being an advocate for the organization and the membership, and building the board-staff partnership.

A. Advancing the Vision

The board of directors is the keeper of the vision. A vision has impact when the organization's members embrace it and are motivated to action.

(Insert your organization's vision statement.)

1. The board understands
   and embraces the vision.   5   4   3   2   1

2. The board uses the vision
as the standard against
which strategic and
policy decisions are made.   5   4   3   2   1

3. Directors assist the
membership to understand
and support the vision.   5   4   3   2   1

B. Promoting the Mission

The board of directors is responsible for clearly defining the mission.

(Insert your organization's mission statement.)

4. The board understands
and supports the
organization's mission.   5   4   3   2   1

5. The board reviews the
mission on a regular basis.   5   4   3   2   1

6. Integral to the mission is
a commitment to be a
multicultural organization.   5   4   3   2   1

C. Strategic Planning

The board of directors is responsible for engaging in a planning process that results in an enhanced understanding of the changing environment in which the organization operates and decisions that will help the organization function more effectively in that environment.

7. The board ensures an
effective strategic planning
process is in place.   5   4   3   2   1

8. The board focuses its
attention on strategic and
policy issues rather than
on operational issues.   5   4   3   2   1

9. The board makes strategic
decisions that are responsive
to trends and other changes
in the environment.   5   4   3   2   1

10. The board devotes sufficient
time to strategic issues.   5   4   3   2   1

D. Fiscal Management

The board of directors is responsible for maintaining sound fiscal policy and practices.

11. The board understands
    its fiduciary responsibility.   5   4   3   2   1

12. The board receives
    sufficient information to
    keep current on the
    organization's financial
    condition and to make
    informed and prudent
    fiscal decisions.   5   4   3   2   1

13. The board makes resource
    allocation decisions that
    enable the organization
    to advance its vision and
    achieve its strategic goals.   5   4   3   2   1

14. The board approves an
    annual operating budget
    established against the
    strategic plan.   5   4   3   2   1

E. Programs and Services

The board of directors is responsible for determining the spectrum of programs and services that should be offered to advance the organization's vision, fulfill its mission, and meet members' needs.

15. The board reviews the
    spectrum of programs
    and services annually to
    be certain they support
    the mission and are
    consistent with the
    strategic plan.   5   4   3   2   1

16. The board receives
    adequate information on
    members' needs, expectations,
    and satisfaction to make
    decisions about programs
    and services.   5   4   3   2   1

F. Advocacy

The board of directors is responsible for enhancing the organization's image and fostering a clear understanding of the organization, its direction, and leadership decisions among the membership and various publics.

17. The board approves a public relations and marketing strategy.	5	4	3	2	1
18. The board fosters effective and open communications between the organization's leadership and membership.	5	4	3	2	1
19. The board designates the official spokespersons for the organization.	5	4	3	2	1

G. Board-Staff Partnership

The board of directors is responsible for building and nurturing an effective working partnership with the staff and in particular with the chief staff executive.

20. The board ensures a climate of mutual trust, and respect exists between the board and the chief staff executive.	5	4	3	2	1
21. The board gives the chief staff executive the authority and responsibility to lead and manage the organization successfully.	5	4	3	2	1
22. The board and the chief staff executive have agreed on how to define success for the organization, and the chief staff executive is evaluated on related criteria.	5	4	3	2	1
23. The board seeks and respects the opinion and recommendations of staff.	5	4	3	2	1

Comments_____

_____

_____

II. BOARD EFFECTIVENESS

Assess how effective and efficient the board is in doing its work. Contributing to effective governance are the following factors: clearly defined roles and responsibilities, an efficient governance structure, well-developed group process, and meaningful meetings.

A. Roles and Responsibilities

24. The board has defined a role for itself.	5	4	3	2	1
25. There is a job description for directors.	5	4	3	2	1
26. Directors execute their responsibilities.	5	4	3	2	1

B. Governance Structure

27. The structure of the board contributes to its ability to function effectively.	5	4	3	2	1
28. Each section, committee, and task force has a charge and is reviewed regularly.	5	4	3	2	1

C. Board Dynamics

29. There is a climate of mutual respect and trust among directors and between directors and staff.	5	4	3	2	1
30. Directors fully participate in board discussions.	5	4	3	2	1
31. Directors have sufficient opportunity to express themselves on issues during board discussions.	5	4	3	2	1
32. There is a clear commitment to building consensus on issues.	5	4	3	2	1

33. The board makes decisions on the basis of information and data about members' needs and satisfaction.	5	4	3	2	1
34. There is effective and appropriate communication between the board and its officers and between the board and the chief staff executive.	5	4	3	2	1

D. Meaningful Meetings

35. Directors receive agendas and supporting materials for review prior to board meetings.	5	4	3	2	1
36. Board meetings make the most productive use of directors' time.	5	4	3	2	1
37. Sufficient meeting time is allowed for reaching consensus on issues.	5	4	3	2	1
38. Board members are familiar with the organization's bylaws.	5	4	3	2	1

Comments

_____

_____

_____

III. BOARD DEVELOPMENT

Assess how committed the organization's board of directors is to preparing new directors for their responsibilities and improving the effectiveness and efficiency of the board.

A. New Directors

39. The current board contains a sufficient range of expertise and experience to make it an effective governing body, representative of the membership.

    5   4   3   2   1

40. Directors help identify candidates for leadership roles in the organization.

    5   4   3   2   1

41. A formal orientation program for new directors is in place.

    5   4   3   2   1

B. Board Development

42. The board commits time for group learning experiences designed to improve the board's effectiveness as a governing body and its understanding of governance issues.

    5   4   3   2   1

43. Directors are encouraged to enhance their individual leadership skills.

    5   4   3   2   1

Comments

_____

_____

_____

IV. GENERAL ASSESSMENT

44. What issues require the board's special attention during the next twelve to twenty-four months?

_____

_____

_____

45. How can the board's structure or performance be improved in the next twelve to twenty-four months?

_____

_____

_____

46. What other comments or suggestions would you like to offer about the board or its performance?

_____

_____

_____

Signature (voluntary)

INDEX

A

Accountability, and ethics, 120–121
Adamson, R., 60–61, 123, 133
American Evaluation Association, 146
American Society of Association Executives, 161, 164
Aramony, W., 120
Aspen Institute, 133
Association for Healthcare Philanthropy, 110
Axelrod, S., 106, 112

B

Beer, M., 94
Behavior Research Center, 121
Belk, J., 60, 113
Board: annual meeting and report of, 42 applications for, 33–36; aspects of coevaluation for, 31–44; background on, 31–32; clients on, 57–58; composition of, 34; evaluation of meetings of, 37–38, 40–42, 159–160; governance assessments for, 161–171; individual members of, 43; information from, 13; and information management, 101; learning reports for, 32–33, 42; meetings of, 36, 37–38, 40–42; and organizational effects, 32–33; Questioning Agenda for, 8–10, 36–37; and resource development, 107, 109; responsibilities of, 35–36; retreats for, 38–39; steps for, 36–43; summary on, 43–44; volunteers on, 47–48
Brudney, J. L., 94
Buchanan, P., 60, 104
Buhl, L. C., 96, 97, 102
Burke, J., 116

C

Change, and organizational effectiveness, 70
Charles Stewart Mott Foundation, 134
Chisolm, L. B., 122
CIPP model, 142
Clients: aspects of coevaluation for, 53–58; aware, 54–55; background on, 53–54; on board, 57–58; information from, 13; steps for, 54–58; summary on, 58
Coevaluation: applying, 1–58; approach for ongoing, 3–21; areas for, 59–147; background on, 3–4; and board, 31–44; and clients, 53–58; concept of, 3–4; and consultants, 140–147; context for, 5–6; and culture, 123–139; definition, xx; development of, 148–158; elements of, 1, 67–68; and ethics, 113–122; and human resource management, 85–94; and information management, 95–103; and leadership, 22–24; as learning, 4–21, 64–67; learning moments in, 7–11; and organizational effectiveness, 63–73;

overviews on, 1–2, 59–61; by participant-evaluators, 141–146; principles of, 21; process for, 6–21; and program effectiveness, 74–84; questions asked in, 6–11; reactions to, 19, 21; and resistance, 21; and resource development, 104–112; responsibility for, 5; results of, 4; rigor in, 72; by staff, 22–30; and success stories, 2; and volunteers, 45–52. *See also* Evaluation

Cohen, E., 96, 98, 102

Commitment: by board, 34; and coevaluation, 19; cultural, 124, 125

Communication: of ethics and values, 117–118; and information management, 100–101

Community Health Worker programs, 99

Confidentiality, in information management, 101

Consultants: aspects of using, 140–147; background on, 140–141; and meta-evaluation, 145; and organizational culture, 133–134; and reflection, 144–145; roles for, 141–145; selecting, 145–146; summary on, 146

Context: for coevaluation, 5–6; for information sharing, 144; for program effectiveness, 74–76

Costa, N. G., 110, 112

Council for Advancement and Support of Education, 110

Council on Foundations, 133

Culture, organizational: adapting evaluation to, 123–139; background on, 123; case study of, 126–137; and information management, 99–100; literature review on, 124–126; summary on, 137–138

D

Daigneault, M., 60, 113

Doermann, H., 60, 85

E

Effectiveness. *See* Organizational effectiveness; Program effectiveness

Empowerment: from culture, 128; from information collection, 14; from learning, 65

Environment, as nurturing for coevaluation, 4–5

Ethics: and accountability, 120–121; aspects of, 113–122; and board retreat, 39; choices in, 113–116; comprehensive approach for, 116–117; dialogues on, 115; guidance on, 119–120; and organizational integrity, 117–121; and success, 121–122. *See also* Values

Ethics, Inc., 122

Ethics Resource Center, 121

Evaluation: difficulties of, 66–67, 73; meta-, 145; naturalistic, 68; normative, 67; responsive, 67–68. *See also* Coevaluation

Evaluators, outside. *See* Consultants

Excellence, searching for, 9

F

Feedback: from clients, 56–57; in information sharing, 16, 18; timely, 65

Fine, G. A., 124, 138

First Nations Development Institute (FNDI): and control of assets, 127–128, 130, 131–132, 134; Development Wheel of, 126–128, 129, 134, 137; Eagle Staff Fund of, 132–137; evaluations by, 126–137; and kinship, 127–128, 130, 132, 134; and personal efficacy, 127–128, 131, 132, 134; and spirituality, 127–128, 131, 132, 134; staff performance at, 129–132; work of, 123

Fisher, L. R., 19, 21

Ford Foundation, 134

Funding: and information management, 98, 101; learning moments in reports on, 11. *See also* Resource development

G

Gray, S. T., 1, 31, 44, 63n, 73, 84, 96, 103, 122, 148, 159

Greater Albion Habitat for Humanity, 98

Greenfield, J. M., 109, 112

H

Haas, R., 115

Hatry, H., 73

Henry, R. C., 100, 103

Hitachi Foundation, 134

Hodgkinson, V. A., 94

Hollister, R. M., 94

Howard, G. S., 124, 138

Howe, F., 109, 112

Hughes, D., 124, 138

Human capital concept, 85

Human resource management: aspects of, 85–94; background on, 85; and co-evaluation, 87–91; of individuals, 86, 87, 88–89; levels of, 86–87; and organizational capacity, 86, 87, 90–91; of staff and volunteers, 91–93; summary on, 93; of teams, 86, 87, 89–90; and workforce diversity, 86–87, 93

Hurwitz, T., 60, 104

I

Impacts, and program effectiveness, 83

Inclusiveness, and organizational effectiveness, 70–71

INDEPENDENT SECTOR, 75, 96, 107, 146

Indiana University Foundation, 107

Information collecting: aspects of, 11–14; by board, 37, 39, 43; by clients, 55, 56, 57–58; by consultants, 143; and culture, 135–136; sources for, 12–13; by staff, 25, 29–30; by volunteers, 46, 48, 51

Information management: aspects of, 95–103; background on, 95–96; barriers to, 101–102; concept of, 96; elements of, 99–101; importance of, 96–99; summary on, 102

Information sharing and using: aspects of, 14–21; by boards, 37–38, 39, 43; by clients, 55–56, 57–58; by consultants, 143–144; Questioning Agenda for, 16–17; by staff, 25, 29–30; summarizing for, 15; by volunteers, 46, 48, 51

Institute for Nonprofit Organization Management, 122

Interpretation panel, 144

J

Johnson & Johnson, 116

Joint Committee on Standards of Educational Evaluation, 145, 147

Joyce Foundation, 126

K

Kellogg Foundation, W. K., 95, 97–98, 134

Kirkhart, K. E., 124, 125, 138

Kleinman, S., 124, 138

Klitgaard, R., 124, 138–139

Knauft, E. B., 31, 44

Kolb, C., 120

L

Lawry, R., 117

Leadership: and coevaluation, 22–24; and organizational effectiveness, 69

Learning: coevaluation as, 4–21, 64–67; concepts of, 19, 21; continuous, and culture, 135, 136–137; moments for, 7–11; reports on, for board, 32–33, 42

Lelle, M., 60, 95

Levi Strauss & Company, 115, 118

Levi Strauss Foundation, 126, 134

Lowery, W. R., 111, 112

M

Mair, M., 124, 139

Management. *See* Human resource management; Information management

Marketing surveys, 68

Mayer, S. E., 53, 58

Merget, A., 59, 63

Millet, R., 60, 72, 73, 95

Mission. *See* Vision and mission

N

National Society of Fund Raising Executives, 110, 112

Newsletters, for volunteers, 49

O

On Purpose Associates, 134

Ooms, T., 96, 98, 102

Operation G.R.A.D., 97

Organizational effectiveness: aspects of, 63–73; and coevaluation, 63–68; conclusion on, 73; imperatives for, 69–71; measuring, 64; and organizational attributes, 68–73; tasks for, 71–73

Outcomes, and program effectiveness, 82–84

Outputs, and program effectiveness, 82

P

Paine, L. S., 122

Partnership, in evaluation, 68

Patrizi, P., 61, 140

Pearce, D. W., 85, 94

Petrie, H. G., 139

Planning: communications on, 19; information for, 16, 19–20; learning moments in, 10; by staff, 30

Program effectiveness: aspects of, 74–84; background and context for, 74–76; elements of, 76–81; and implementation issues, 76–81; measuring, 83–84; and results, 81–84; summary on, 84

Putnam, R. S., 124, 139

Q

Questioning Agenda: for board, 8–10, 36–37; for information sharing, 16–17; for volunteers, 48

Questions: aspects of asking, 6–11; by boards, 37, 39, 43; by clients, 54, 55–56, 57; by consultants, 142; information from, 11–14; in information management, 100; on program effectiveness, 77–81; by staff, 25, 29–30; on standard procedures, 7–8; by volunteers, 46, 48, 51

R

Reflection, and consultants, 144–145
Research, learning moments in internal, 11
Resource development: aspects of, 104–112; background on, 104–105; budget adequacy for, 108; businesslike, 109–111; and core processes, 110; process for, 105–108; responsibility for, 111. *See also* Funding
Retreats: board, 38–39; volunteer, 49
Rion, M., 114, 122

S

Sanders, J. R., 61, 96, 103, 140, 145, 147
Schein, E. H., 124–125, 139
Seeley, J., 59–60, 74
Seidman, E., 124, 138
Senge, P., 19, 21
Simic, C. R., 107
Spector, B., 94
Staff: annual assessment of, 88–89; aspects of coevaluation for, 22–30; human resource management of, 91–93; as individuals, 24–25; and information management, 101; leadership by, 23–24; learning moments for, 8; meetings of, 8, 28–30; performance evaluation for, 129–132; recruiting, 88; and resource development, 107–108, 109; at retirement or termination, 89; summary on, 28; and volunteers, 27, 49; in work groups, 26–28
Stockdill, S. H., 14, 21, 122
Stoehr, M., 14, 21
Structure, for organizational effectiveness, 69–70
Sumariwalla, R. D., 64, 68, 73
Systems thinking models, 142

T

Taylor, M. E., 64, 68, 73
Trust, climate of, 23, 68, 69

U

United Way of America, 120–121

V

Values: and clients, 55; and culture, 124–125; and staff, 24, 26; and volunteers, 50. *See also* Ethics
Vision and mission: and board, 34; and clients, 55; and staff, 24, 26; and volunteers, 49–50
Volunteers: aspects of coevaluation for, 45–52; background on, 45–46; on board, 47–48; human resource management of, 91–93; information from, 13; and information management, 101; meetings of, 48; and questioning, 7–8; and resource development, 107; retaining, 46–47; retreats for, 49; and staff, 27, 49; starter questions for, 49–51; steps for, 48–49; summary on, 51–52

W

Waldrop, M. M., 67, 73
Weaver, E. T., 59, 60–61, 63, 123
Williams, N., 124, 138
Worthen, B. R., 145, 147

Y

Young, D. R., 60, 85, 94